WHEN *the* DIAMONDS WERE GONE

A Jewish Refugee Comes of Age in America in the 1940s

JULIAN PADOWICZ

ACADEMY

CHICAGO

Copyright © 2015 by Julian Padowicz
All rights reserved

First edition
Published by Academy Chicago Publishers
An imprint of Chicago Review Press Incorporated
814 North Franklin Street
Chicago, Illinois 60610

ISBN 978-0-89733-919-3

Library of Congress Cataloging-in-Publication Data
Padowicz, Julian, author.
When the diamonds were gone : a Jewish refugee comes of age
in America in the 1940s / Julian Padowicz. — First edition.
    pages cm
ISBN 978-0-89733-919-3 (paperback)
1. Padowicz, Julian—Childhood and youth. 2. Jews—New York (State)—
New York—Biography. 3. Jews, Polish—New York (State)—New
York—Biography. 4. Young men—New York (State)—New York—
Biography. 5. Boarding school students—Biography. 6. Mothers and
sons—New York (State)—New York. I. Title.
F128.9.J5P33 2015
306.874'3--dc23
                                    2015001374

Cover design: Sarah Olson
Cover photographs: Sean Justice/Getty Images
Interior design: Nord Compo
Printed in the United States of America
5 4 3 2 1

To my Uncle Arthur and Aunt Julia Szyk
and
Professor Jonathan and Patricia Kistler
each of whom nurtured me in his or her own way

Acknowledgments

Neither this book nor any of its predecessors would have been possible without the help and encouragement of my lovely wife, Donna.

Prologue

This is the fourth and, probably, the last segment of my memoir. Of course, when I was writing the third segment, *Loves of Yulian* about our stay in Brazil, I thought it to be the last. And for that matter, when I was writing the first one, *Mother and Me: Escape from Warsaw 1939*, I didn't think I would be doing a sequel. *Mother and Me*, with its trek over the Carpathian Mountains into neutral Hungary, had such a perfect climax that I thought anything that came after it would be anticlimactic.

But as I thought over our stays in Hungary and, later, Brazil I realized that each of those also had drama and a climax. A very different kind of drama, but a drama nevertheless. Those experiences became *A Ship in the Harbor* followed by *Loves of Yulian*, which taught me, as a writer, to look beyond the obvious. And thus I came to realize that the story of an insecure, war-damaged kid plopped into the American educational system, struggling to catch up and trying to live up to his overachiever mother's demands, was not just my quirky childhood but a veritable drama of its own.

So this book came to be. It ends with my graduating college and moving out into an adult world I had come to believe was out of my reach. This climax is certainly not the end of my story. Getting from that callow college graduate to where I now sit, inputting into my laptop the events of my life, has the stuff of several more dramas. But those are stories involving persons now living whose privacy I don't wish to disturb. That I have already imposed on the privacy of several of my peers I take very seriously. I believe that I have not treated anyone unfairly and, frankly, it took considerable editing, on my own initiative, to assure myself of this fact. After this, I will stick strictly to fiction.

Chapter One

I recognized Uncle Arthur's bald head from the deck as our ship came to its excruciatingly slow stop at the dock in New York. Uncle Arthur was my favorite uncle by virtue of having been the one person whose French I had been able to understand when I attended first grade in a French school before the start of the war. That had been some three years earlier, in Warsaw, Poland, and I had spoken no French going in and only a few words coming out. It would be years before Mother explained to me that Uncle Arthur had, actually, just been speaking to me in Polish with a burlesque French accent.

But now a war was raging across Europe. The French school, our home, and the park that my nanny and I had visited daily were probably all gone, and the gangplank that the stevedores were already lifting into position against the still moving hull was about to become the final link in my mother's and my nineteen-month odyssey from the terror of German bombs to safety and, I dearly hoped, normalcy.

I remembered Uncle Arthur as a small, roly-poly man with a round, bald head, a round body, and small hands who played the piano and said things that made grown-ups laugh. But, most importantly to me, Uncle Arthur was a painter of pictures. Before the war, he and Aunt Julia had been living in Paris, where most artists lived.

They had come to New York just a year before our own arrival, and we would be staying with them until we got settled. Mother and "Uncle" Arthur were first cousins, their mothers having been sisters, making him, in reality, my first cousin once removed.

Just how we were to "get settled" was a mystery to me since my beautiful socialite mother, Barbara, Warsaw's *Beautiful Basia,* could neither read nor write in English, couldn't type, cook, or sew, and had never held a commercial position. We had financed our travel across Europe, to Brazil, and now to New York by the gradual sale of the diamonds Mother had sewn into her clothing when the Soviets first occupied the part of Poland we had fled to when the bombing of Warsaw began. But except for the one remaining diamond in Mother's engagement ring and a round diamond broach of my grandmother's that was of great sentimental value but little monetary worth, the stones were all gone. I dearly hoped that Uncle Arthur's paintings were better appreciated here in America than they had been in France.

Some nineteen months earlier, my beloved nanny, Kiki, had gone home to her own family and my stepfather, Lolek, had put on his reserve officer's uniform and gone to the barracks. On the second night of the war we felt the shock of bombs landing around us, and Mother and I left Warsaw, heading away from the attacking Germans. We had traveled in the back of one of the large, windowless delivery vans from Lolek's shirt factory along with two of my aunts and two young cousins. After a few days, we found ourselves in the rural southeast of Poland where, two weeks later, the Soviet army marched in, unopposed, while our own army fought the Germans on the west. We went on to spend the next six months living under harsh Soviet occupation.

As food, firewood, and medical supplies grew scarce and the authorities oppressive, my mother proved to be what I would later hear people call *resourceful, creative*, and *courageous* in providing for our needs. With her glamorous dyed-blonde looks, her charm, her fluent Russian (my grandmother was Russian), and a quality I would later learn to call *chutzpah*, Mother had managed to win special favors from the authorities. We had small quantities of sausage and firewood when these were not available to the rest of the population. What it had also achieved was great embarrassment on my part and disapproval of her methods.

Disapproving of Mother's methods had been a major occupation of mine at the time, and to understand it we must go back once more to the prewar period and consider two things. With a crucifix and a photograph of her "mother in heaven" on the wall over her bed, the rosary beads and little prayer book with the gold-edged pages in her purse, the gold cross on a chain around her neck, and her Sunday attendance at mass, Kiki, my beloved nanny, was Roman Catholic, whereas I and my parents were Jewish. We had no photographs of Moses or prayer books or stars of David. We never went to synagogue. But the real difference was that Kiki was headed for heaven, and we were not. It wasn't that we were any more sinful, though we probably were since Kiki did not sin, or that we didn't practice our Jewish religion, but simply the fact that heaven was exclusive to Catholics. I had Kiki's word on that.

But Kiki, with her *real* blonde braids wound around her head and a face innocent of makeup, loved me. And, because of that love, she taught me to recite the *Our Father* and the *Hail Mary*, to perform the sign of the cross, and to say the rosary. She also described to me the disgraceful things my people had done to God's son, Jesus, which, like the recent Last War that Kiki told me about, I had been born too late to witness. Whether they had happened in Kiki's lifetime I wasn't sure, though from her detailed description I suspected they must have. If I were truly, truly sorry for these misdeeds, if I continued reciting my prayers every night, and if I were at some future time to be baptized, I had Kiki's virtual guarantee that, one day, I would be joining her in the presence of God, his wife, Mary, and their boy, Jesus. Jesus, I understood, was back in heaven now and a little boy again. How these things worked, I didn't want to question, which I understood to be the proper Catholic attitude.

Kiki had been my entire life, and when on the second morning of the war I had woken up to find her gone and my mother seated at our little green table in a cloud of cigarette smoke, waiting to tell me to get dressed and go to the kitchen where Marta, our cook, would wash me and give me breakfast, my life had derailed for the second time.

The first time my life had derailed was just one year earlier, in the fall of 1938. In Poland, you see, schoolchildren wore uniforms. The boys wore navy blue with shiny metal buttons on the jacket and long trousers with stripes down the side. The color of the stripe indicated which school you attended. And all this splendor was topped by a peaked cap with braid and a shiny visor. On holidays, students would march in parades along with soldiers, keeping step to band music and carrying flags. Kiki and I had watched them from our apartment window, and the ultimate ambition of my pre-school life was to become one of that number. I could not wait for the summer of 1938 to end so that we could get back from our beach resort and I could be fitted for my new uniform.

Then, on our return to Warsaw, Kiki and I were both informed that the school I would be attending was a French school whose uniform, in the French style, was a black smock with a white Peter Pan collar and a black beret. It had been, by a large margin, the worst news I had received to date. What saved it from being the total disaster it might have been was the fact that, blessedly, the French school did not participate in Polish parades.

Until the start of the war and Kiki's disappearance from my life, my mother had been a glittering presence at the far edge of my reality. Only the French school business had made me aware that such a person as Mother actually had influence over my life. There she had stepped in with her spike heel and turned every one of my hopes and dreams into mush. Though eighteen months later she would lead the two of us through the snow-covered Carpathian Mountains in an against-all-warnings escape from Soviet occupation into "neutral" Hungary and eventually to safety in the United States, from that moment on a certain edge of distrust and disapproval of Mother's methods had always been present in the back of my mind. My mother wasn't like other mothers.

Now in the harbor in New York I could see that below us a woman, who must have been Aunt Julia under her hat and veil, was holding Uncle Arthur's elbow with one hand and waving enthusiastically with the other. A second, younger woman had her arm hooked through my uncle's other elbow and waved with equal zeal. Her I construed to be Cousin Alice, about whose existence I knew but whom I could not remember meeting.

"Oh look, Yulian, there are Uncle Arthur, Aunt Julia, and, oh, I bet that must be Alice. See how she's grown?" my mother said in Polish, pointing with her hand. "There, see? To the left of the man in the army uniform. See them? In front of that woman with the fox stole. Can you see them? They're waving—wave back."

I raised my hand a little above the railing and moved it back and forth, in grudging compliance. I was not given to exuberant expression of excessive emotion. And Mother's assuming that I needed to have Uncle Arthur pointed out to me, when I had spotted him long before she did, had definitely affected my willingness to concede any prerogatives. I was nine years old, and these things were important to me.

"Oh, isn't this wonderful, Yulian!" Mother enthused. "We've made it! We've finally arrived! We're in America! America, Yulian! Can you believe it? Aren't you excited?"

I nodded my head. In fact, I *was* excited, but for my own reasons. That excitement had been somewhat dampened when Mother had dragged me on deck at an ungodly hour of the morning to look at some dumb statue in the harbor. Then she had sat me down on my bed in our cabin and repeated the admonition she had leveled at me some months earlier in Brazil: "Yulian, you are never, ever to say to anyone that we are Jewish." In her eyes I had seen not the logic in which she normally tried to dress her pronouncements, but a strangely naked fear that her very life hung on some chance utterance of mine.

There had been good reason for such fear back in Europe. Though we had never found ourselves under the authority of the homicidal Nazis, a prevailing anti-Semitism had been discernable in the chance remarks of people we had met along our journey. In Brazil, where Jewish people had freely proclaimed their Jewishness with no apparent consequences, I had thought Mother's continuing concern misdirected. Here in America where, according to the presentation we had been given on the ship, freedom of religion was cherished and even black Africans were left to their own beliefs as long as they kept to their own bathrooms and drinking fountains, I would have called her concern *paranoid*, had that word been in my vocabulary.

Along with my mother and me at the railing of our ship was my friend Meesh. Meesh was a white teddy bear who had begun life as my son a year and a half ago in Soviet-occupied Lvoof. He and I had become inseparable, and I had taken him everywhere in the crook of my elbow. He had crossed the Carpathian Mountains in my backpack. But over the months, our relationship had evolved to that of friends, with Meesh spending most days sitting on my bed when Mother and I went out and nights either on a chair beside my bed or, when Mother left me alone in our hotel room, in bed with me. This morning, however, after some deliberation, I had determined that even though he no longer cared to go out into the street with me, it would be unfair not to give him the opportunity to view our arrival in America with us.

But now that I could see my Uncle Arthur almost directly below us, waving quietly in the midst of the noisy crowd, I was reminded of what awaited me in America. Uncle Arthur was an artist, and artists employed *models*— ladies who, I knew, posed for them without any clothes on. Unlike other people, these ladies apparently didn't at all mind being seen naked by other people and could thus be willing to satisfy a recently acquired interest of mine.

In Rio, Mother and I had met a Polish woman, Irenka, who was younger and even more beautiful than Mother. She had frequently accompanied me to the beach, where she would lie on her stomach and unbutton the straps of her bathing suit, presenting a clear view of the side of her plump, white breast, inches from my eyes. Sometimes, as she changed position, a pink nipple would appear momentarily. For some reason, this had awakened a powerful interest in seeing the rest of Irenka, as well as the female anatomy in general, and in Uncle Arthur's studio this interest might well be satisfied.

The downside of settling in America, of course, was that I would have to attend school. The one year I had spent in that French school in Warsaw had been a miserable experience. My classmates all had French parents and spoke the language at home. Things had been shouted at me in ascending decibels and titters had erupted at my inability to comprehend instruction. I had been pushed, pinched, and tripped by invisible appendages, and even shoved down the stairs as we headed for outdoor recess. On numerous occasions I would hear my name mentioned in the middle of a French conversation between one of my fellow students and the teacher, followed by the teacher's ordering, "Padowicz, *danz le coin!*" This phrase I did learn by heart to mean "Padowicz, into the corner." I would trudge to the corner and stand there in shame over my unknown transgression.

At that point, I had thought the fault to be my ignorance of the French language, but my experience in a Brazilian school in Rio de Janeiro, where I did have command of several words of the language, had brought to light some further qualities of mine that contributed to my difficulties. Getting along with other children required skills that I now knew I lacked. On the ship between Lisbon and Brazil twin brothers from Holland had even tried to push me overboard. But, fortunately, this was May and I reasoned that before another school term began, I should have amassed enough English to at least eliminate the language problem.

It turned out that my uncle and aunt had a comfortable apartment occupying the entire top floor of a five-story brownstone on West Seventy-Fourth Street, just near Riverside Drive along the Hudson River. It had a second bedroom, into which Mother and I were settled for the time being. In the living room there were double glass doors that opened out onto the roof of the adjoining four-story building, making it their private terrace. As I had hoped, Uncle Arthur's paintings seemed to be quite well received in America.

What Uncle Arthur's home did not have was a studio with easels, canvases, brushes, or ladies who modeled. To my great disappointment, Uncle Arthur's work space was one very large desk with hundreds of little bottles filled with different colored inks or paints. He had pens, pencils with long, well-sharpened leads, and crayons, a large magnifying glass, and thin brushes that came to an even thinner point. And what he drew and painted were not real people, but caricatures and cartoons of Adolf Hitler, Benito Mussolini, and other scruffy, Germanic-looking characters. I found them very funny in an ugly sort of way, and, apparently, so did many people in America since his cartoons, I soon learned, appeared on the covers of leading magazines. But there wasn't a naked lady among them.

That I should be so grossly disappointed was something over which I took myself to task the very night following my discovery. Thinking back to the business of school uniforms in Warsaw, my rejection by my French-speaking schoolmates, the sudden disappearance of the only mother figure I had ever known, and the Dutch twins I had tried to befriend on the ship trying to push me overboard, I realized that disappointment was what I was destined for. Some people, like Mother, reached out for things and achieved them. I, on the other hand, would only have the satisfaction of imagining good things.

Before the war my uncle, Arthur Szyk, I now learned, had made a career of painting exquisitely detailed miniatures to illustrate books and historical events. And because our family was Jewish, most of Uncle Arthur's paintings had to do with Jewish history—though his series of little paintings depicting the American Revolution hung in the White House. But when Hitler began persecuting the Jews a few years earlier, Uncle Arthur had laid aside his book and history illustrating and turned his work to depicting Nazi atrocities through his weapon of choice: a penetrating, venomous wit. He had, in fact, come to the United States specifically with a mission to make America aware of what was happening in Europe. Over the ensuing years, Uncle Arthur's lethal caricatures would adorn the pages and covers of America's most popular magazines, as well as the halls of prestigious exhibition galleries. They also filled two books, *The New Order* and *Ink and Blood.*

By an interesting coincidence, Mother had come to America with a similar mission. Mother's mission to alert America, however, was motivated from a different paradigm. In the Carpathian village where we had found shelter, some fourteen months before, sleep deprived and euphoric over our successful escape from the Bolsheviks, Mother had said to me, "When we reach America, Yulian, I will write a book and become famous and rich." Later that same day, sitting in the office of a Hungarian border security officer, she had told the man how she planned to write a tell-all book acquainting the American people with the atrocities that were being perpetrated by the Soviets and the Nazis occupying our country. The following day, in Budapest, when Mother's prewar friends were celebrating her heroic escape, a Polish intelligence officer had reminded us that "neutral" Hungary was, in fact, a Nazi-sympathizing country and the authorities were not about to permit Mother to reach America with her book ideas.

The man had tried to get us to conceal ourselves in a safe house the Polish embassy maintained until a passport could be issued under a different name and entry into a more neutral country arranged. But Mother had balked at this interruption of her newfound celebrity and refused his offer, much to my concern, and we had ended up playing a game of hide-and-seek with the authorities.

Some months later, in Rio de Janeiro, Brazil, we had met Sr. Ernesto Segiera, who wanted Mother to marry him and stay in Brazil. Of the many men who had made such proposals to Mother during our travels, Sr. Ernesto was the first whom I could tell that Mother really liked. And I had been all for her marrying him—not only did I like him, but also he had a son my age with whom I actually got along. But Mother had had her heart set on writing her book in America, and we had said a sad goodbye to Sr. Ernesto on the dock in Rio. Now that we were in America, how Mother intended to follow through on her boast of a book was beyond me, since she could neither read nor write the English language.

In addition, I could see that our presence in Uncle and Aunt's apartment was not a permanent solution to our needs. Mother and I occupied what had been Cousin Alice's room and Alice, nineteen years old and engaged, now had to sleep on the living room sofa. Virtually out of diamonds now, my commercially challenged Mother would have to find a way for us to make our own living in America, and my concern over our future was matched only by my curiosity over how all this might be accomplished.

Introducing Mother to her New York acquaintances must have been a bit of a lark for my aunt, since reports of our dramatic escape had, apparently, preceded us to the refugee community in the city. A number of old friends and relatives from Poland who had managed to get out before the border was sealed by the army had made their way to New York. We were the only ones who had stayed to experience the occupation and then escaped.

In addition, Mother was already well-known, by reputation, to many of the Polish element for her celebrated beauty as well as for some, mysterious to me, scandal in her home town of Lodz, related in some way to my father's mysterious death when I was one year old. For many of her new friends, drinking martinis with *Beautiful Basia Waisbrem* of Warsaw, the notorious *Widow Padowicz* of Lodz, and the celebrated heroine of the Carpathian Mountains, all in the same person, must have been an awe-inspiring experience. And Mother, of course, never tired of telling and retelling our escape story.

Of course, whenever she retold our story it tended to change a little, with my part growing smaller and hers bigger with each repetition. At one point she had me falling into a stream and her pulling me out. Had I, in fact, fallen into a stream and been pulled out, I would have frozen to death. On the other hand, the incident of her getting her leg caught under a log and me using a pole to lever her out disappeared completely.

As to that mysterious Lodz scandal, it was something that had been hidden from me from my earliest days, and the more it was hidden, the more aware of it I became. Lodz was where I was born and where my late father died, and every time my father was mentioned in my presence, all in the room lowered their eyes, nodded their heads, and concurred, almost in chorus, that he had died of a cold.

Now, in those pre-antibiotic days it was quite possible for a person to die of a cold, but there was something in their rehearsed affirmation that had always made me suspicious. Then, the night before our celebrated Carpathian escape, I had overheard Mother discussing with a family friend the fact that my father had shot himself, there in Lodz, and that, somehow, she was believed responsible. Mother didn't know that I had overheard them and on more than one occasion, when I felt myself particularly put upon by my perfectionist mother ("Close that drawer more quietly," "How can you show your face at the table with those dirty nails?" "How do you expect me to go to the store with someone wearing *that* color shirt with *that* color pants?" or, "Gentlemen flush the toilet quietly"), I would ask her to tell me again about my father's death and watch her eyes turn to the floor and her face grow somber as she assured me that he had died of a cold.

Soon after our arrival in New York, I was informed by Mother and Aunt Julia that when summer came I would be attending camp with my cousins, Anita and Andy, whom I knew from Warsaw and who had arrived in New York the year before. The word "camp," which apparently was the same in English as it was in Polish, had only been in my lexicon since our departure from Warsaw. I had acquired it during our stay with the Soviets, when persons considered undesirable by the prevailing order were enclosed behind electrified wire fencing with armed guards and sometimes dogs to prevent their departure. And we all knew that more people went in than ever came back out.

But I was also quite proud of my ability to reason things out and, where another nine-year-old in my position might have jumped to the conclusion that his family was suddenly proposing his disposal, I knew that there must be a more reasonable explanation. Anticipating possible involvement in the European war, I reasoned, America was quite cleverly preparing its young people to deal with the potential conse-quences of an involvement, such as camp incarceration. It was something that certainly had not been done in my own, more primitive country. Undoubtedly, the fences would not *really* be electrified, though the campers would be led to believe that they were, and the guards would be benign local peasants with blank cartridges in their rifles, leading equally benign dogs. And as proof of my conclusions was the fact that Anita and Andy had attended camp the previous summer and were looking forward to returning.

Had I asked either cousin for further description of this camp, I could have saved myself a considerable amount of reasoning. But experience with my foreign-tongued playmates in Poland and Brazil, my secretive mother, and mystery-inclined Kiki had directed me to turning inside for solutions.

Anita's mother, Sophie, whose whereabouts we did not know at the time, was another cousin of my mother and Uncle Arthur's, and Andy was Anita's cousin on her father's side. Anita's father, Maximilian Apfelbaum, Warsaw's leading prewar furrier, had brought Anita, Andy, and Andy's parents out of Poland before the start of the war and had now established himself as Maximilian Furs on New York's Fifty-Seventh Street.

As I waited in the Szyks' front hall for the ring informing us that the car driving Anita, Andy, and me to camp was waiting below, Aunt Julia held a reassuring arm around Mother's shoulders. "Aren't you bringing Meesh with you?" she suddenly asked me.

I said that I wasn't. I did not want to have to tell her that he and I had actually discussed it the day before, and I had explained to Meesh that he would not enjoy camp. And then Mother suddenly took me by the hand and led me back into our bedroom. At first I thought we were going to retrieve Meesh, but Mother seated herself on her bed and, taking both my hands in hers, directed her round, brown eyes straight into mine with the gravest concern.

"Yulian, I want you to swear something to me, on your honor as a soldier," she said.

For some reason, whenever something of consequence was required of me, I became either a soldier or a knight. I mumbled agreement.

"I want you to take an officer's oath that you will not tell one single person in camp that you are Jewish," she said. "Some boys will suspect that you are because, in the bathroom, they will see your . . . your nose . . . but you tell them that in Poland a lot of Catholics have noses like that."

Since she was holding both my hands I couldn't raise my right hand to make it official, which was just as well. While I had no intention of discussing either my spiritual issues or my organs with anybody, complicated as they were, I preferred not to be betting my honor against some inadvertent disclosure. And particularly since my cousins Anita and Andy seemed to make no effort to conceal their Judaism, my Semitic ethnicity would certainly be assumed. "I so swear," I said, and watched great relief come over Mother's face.

Then Aunt Julia knocked on the door to say that my ride was downstairs, and Mother admonished me that gentlemen didn't keep people waiting.

There was no fence around Camp Pinewood—located a few hours away in a state to the east of New York with an unpronounceable name—and no guards, so I didn't see how it qualified to be called a camp. It was a large clearing beside a lake in an evergreen woods with cabins that they called *bunks*, and various athletic fields. There was a variety of activities you could pursue, including canoeing, swimming, hiking, tennis, and baseball.

Baseball was a game that I had a very hard time getting my head around. All the team games that I was familiar with, whether it was soccer, hockey, or basketball, consisted of a goal of one kind or another that you had to defend and another goal, at the other end of the field, that you tried to penetrate. Even war worked on that same principle. But in this game they threw a very hard ball called a *softball* at your head while you tried to protect yourself with a club. Then you ran around in a circle and finally ended up where you began, sitting on a bench and watching others play. On top of that, the ball was so hard that it hurt your hand to catch it. Not owning a "mitt," I had, on more than one occasion, intentionally avoided catching it. As for the rules, they were so many and so complicated that I couldn't possibly remember them.

On one rainy afternoon, Mike, the counselor in our bunk, produced two pairs of boxing gloves and proceeded to teach us to box. This got my attention immediately— Mother had told me that someday I would learn to box. All gentlemen knew how to box and to fence, she explained. While I knew that the swords you fenced with had buttons on the ends and that you wore a protective face mask, boxing had no such protections. I was concerned about being hit by the other boxer. But Mother had explained that you didn't try to hurt each other, but rather to score points by making light contact, and the soft boxing gloves absorbed all the impact anyway. And what I found most interesting was her saying that you shook hands before and after each bout and that these bouts didn't create enemies, but actually worked to cement friendships. Young men who boxed each other, she said, did not dislike each other, as you would think, but instead formed a particularly strong bond. The part about boxing creating friendships appealed to me in particular, since I had learned that friends were rare and hard to come by.

My eagerness must have been showing, because Mike selected me as one of the first pair of boxers. My opponent was a boy named Jack who was about my size, told a lot of jokes, and seemed to have a lot of friends. I, of course, with my budding English, didn't usually understand the jokes, but everyone else found them funny and seemed to welcome Jack's company at meals and other activities. Establishing a close and lasting friendship with Jack would be a major step toward being accepted by the other boys in our bunk. Mike could not have selected a better partner for me.

As Jack and I circled each other, following Mike's directions, I found that I could not see Jack's face behind his two gloves. When I swung my head around to one side, to get a view of him, Jack would swing his in the other direction, keeping his gloves a constant barrier between us. This gave me an ingenious idea—I would swing my head to the left, then thrust my right fist to where I could expect his face to appear.

I carried out my plan, felt my fist make solid contact, and heard a howl from my soon-to-be bosom friend. Jack's fists dropped, revealing tears, a bloody nose, and a mouth twisted in sobs. Several of the boys, sitting cross-legged in a circle around us, immediately began to cheer and, as I held out my hand to shake with Jack, began chanting my name.

Jack didn't shake my hand and I don't believe that he or any of his close friends ever spoke to me again. But, somehow, I had earned the admiration of several bunk mates. For the next few days, wherever I went one or two accompanied me, often with an arm around my shoulders. On several occasions one of them had called me over to his locker and given me a chocolate or a cookie, and I had numerous confidences whispered in my ear—which I, unfortunately, could not understand, but to which I learned to hold my mouth a certain way and nod my head.

Actually, communicating nonverbally had become a medium of choice for me, for reasons beyond my ignorance of the English language. Back in Hungary, a year earlier, I had experienced an emotional trauma that left me with a stammer that had made my subsequent efforts at communicating difficult in any language. The words simply would not come out on demand. And the greater the demand, the greater their reluctance. It had been particularly burdensome in the presence of my mother, who made no secret of the embarrassment I was causing her and whose command to "just say it, Yulian!" would put an end to anything I might be trying to communicate. And this phenomenon had, in its turn, resulted in my acceptance of things being left unsaid, of questions left unasked, responses not delivered, and feelings unshared.

In the course of the nine or so months that we had spent in Brazil, I had learned to control this stammer for the most part. By speaking slowly, controlling my emotions, and exerting considerable effort, I could force words out of my mouth so that Mother no longer had much occasion for embarrassment from that direction.

Where I felt the most comfortable at Camp Pinewood was in the water. During our Brazil stay, I had developed into a strong swimmer, and I passed Pinewood's test for deep-water swimming on my first try. Those of us who passed the test used a buddy system that paired you with a partner, and you had to stay within a certain distance of each other at all times while in the deep water. My first buddy was a boy whose name I no longer remember, but we managed to communicate despite my inadequate English and limited experience relating to my peers. But halfway into the summer he developed appendicitis and was taken away in an ambulance in the middle of the night. Because we now had an odd number of boys in my swimming category, I was directed to join an existing pair of buddies as the proverbial third wheel.

It was clear to me that my new buddies—George Bloom, a very tall boy, and Fred Stein, who picked at his face constantly—resented my intrusion into what had apparently developed into a close friendship. At first, George and Fred tried to lose me. When I wasn't watching, they would suddenly swim away, forcing me to chase after them. But this quickly became a game for me, since I could catch them with ease, using any one of four strokes. Sometimes I would pretend to not be paying attention just so we could play our little game.

Fred and George would say things that I didn't understand or hear, and then make fun of my confusion. This of course reminded me of the year in the French school when my classmates found my ignorance of French both disrespectful and amusing. Now, a good deal wiser and aware that my bread was destined to land jam-side down, I did my best to act as though it did not matter to me one little bit.

Then one evening as we walked to our bunk after some activity, my two swimming buddies surprised me by approaching me from both sides and extending an invitation to join them in a clandestine activity after lights out. It seemed that on this night, the girls in the senior bunk would be doing something called "skinny-dipping" in the lake.

I had never heard the term before, but the reference to skin gave me a good idea of its meaning and my interest was immediately aroused. Fred and George said they were planning to sneak out of our bunk and hide in the bushes as clandestine observers, and I was invited to join them. That other boys maintained the same interest in female anatomy as I did was a revelation to me.

Whether I was more excited by the idea of what I would be seeing or by the fact of being invited to join them in a secret activity, I'm not sure to this day. At any rate, by prearranged plan, the three of us made our way out of our bunk some time after lights out by way of an open window screen over Fred's bed and proceeded down the hill to the lakeshore. The girls were not there yet, but my friends assured me they would be there as soon as their own lights out had occurred.

Because I was the recognized senior swimmer of our group, I was told I could have the hiding place nearest to the beach, behind a log from where I would have the closest, least-obstructed view of the night's happenings. And I was instructed to be extremely still and extremely quiet. My two friends would find hiding places somewhere behind me. The moon was bright that night, there was a night light on a pole lighting the canoes rocking gently in their night enclosure, and I was basking in the glow of good fellowship.

I knew now that adults had pubic hair—I had seen it on Mother, as she tried to cover it with her hand, and on Mike, our counselor—and I wondered if these girls would have it as well. Would they have real breasts or just swellings? Would they be coming down naked or taking off their pajamas there on the beach? For some reason, the idea of undressing on the beach seemed the more exciting of the two.

Then I heard a girl's voice somewhere behind me. I waited for someone to appear, but no one did. I didn't hear another voice. I waited.

Then I waited some more. It grew chilly. I wondered what time it was. Looking up the hill, I could not see or hear any activity. Fred and George must have been well hidden behind me, because I could not see them. I knew I must be patient. Good things are worth waiting for.

And then Mike was shaking me awake. He pointed a flashlight at my face, and I could see numerous other counselors down at the water's edge, looking up at us. "What on earth are you doing out here?" Mike was asking.

One of the benefits of being in the company of adults, as I had been for the past year and a half, is that you hear things and learn things. One of the things I had heard, sitting at a sidewalk café in Rio with Mother and two of her Polish friends, was that there was a phenomenon called *sleepwalking*. As a matter of fact, the last few miles of our trek over the Carpathian Mountains I had walked in my sleep, since I had no memory of them. "I . . . I must have walked in my sleep," I explained to Mike.

"Well, let's get you back to bed," Mike said. As we came up to the rear of our bunk, I could see that the window screen through which I and my two friends had made our exit had been closed. Probably by Fred and George. Had I tried to sneak back in by myself, I would have had a difficult time of it.

In the summer of 1941, Britain was fighting for its very survival, as Hitler, having given up his planned invasion of the island, was now trying to strangle the country with his U-boat fleet. In an expression of solidarity with our embattled brethren, we campers were taught to sing "God Save the King." My English had grown considerably in those first weeks, to the extent that I understood almost all of the words in that British anthem. I even reasoned out that *reign* couldn't reasonably mean *rain*.

Where I did have a bit of trouble was with the phrase, "Send him victorious, happy, and glorious." I did not know either the word *victorious* or *glorious* and took them to be proper nouns rather than adjectives. I had heard of Queen Victoria and assumed *Victorious* to be the masculine version of that name, possibly the queen's warrior brother, and *Glorious*, maybe another brother. And, following my logic, I made these two to be historical heroes of some sort who had saved Britain once and were being called on to do it again. In fact I could envision these two legendary warriors, Victorious and Glorious, flanking King George on his throne, in a metaphorical way, with swords, shields, and helmets at the ready. I was proud of my understanding of metaphor, though I didn't know the actual word.

And as for *Happy*, well, every nine-year-old knew that Happy was one of the Seven Dwarves. And any country that derived its inspiration from Walt Disney as well as history could not be conquered by the likes of Adolf Hitler.

Chapter Two

Returning to New York at the end of the summer, I discovered that Mother had rented for us our own apartment on the top floor of the building right next to that of my aunt and uncle. It was the building that was one story shorter than that of the Szyks, so our roof was actually their deck, making for easy transit between our two apartments. During my absence Mother had, apparently, also marched into the offices of Duell, Sloan, and Pearce, book publishers, and either charmed or bullied them into giving her an advance on the book she planned to write. I knew by now that Mother was well capable of either tactic. In addition, since Mother spoke little English and could write not one word, they had given her a "ghost," a professional writer to fashion Mother's story into a book. I had to admit that while Mother was a definite obstruction in my life, there were some things, like this one, that I had to admire her for.

Mother had also made other contacts, people whom she would go to meet in the evenings, leaving me sleeping alone on the sofa of our living room. On occasion people would be coming to our apartment, and then I would have to go up to our roof and into my aunt and uncle's apartment to spend the night on their sofa. These meetings were all for business reasons, Mother explained, though what business she was in exactly was never made clear to me. I did know that Mother always had money to pay our rent, to wear fashionable dresses, and to have her hair done by a hairdresser on the East Side who, she claimed, was the most *fashionable* hairdresser in New York.

Then the dreaded school term began. But I found that it did not have the same terror for me that it had held last spring. If camp had not prepared me for potential wartime incarceration, it did go a long way toward changing my perspective of other children. I had learned to be more cautious in expressing my feelings, to feign appreciation and agreement when I didn't understand a story or a direction, and, above all, to make judicious use of one of my biggest aids, my ignorance of the English language. I had also gained a working knowledge of baseball and learned the secret of pulling my hand back at the same time that I caught the painful ball so as to minimize the impact. And I possessed an asset that had served me well in the past and I knew would serve me again, namely the fact that I could outrun anyone of my age that I had ever raced against. Now I actually found myself look-ing forward to meeting other boys and learning things I didn't know.

There was a private school a few short blocks along Riverside Drive from our apartment, and Mother took me to be enrolled there. As we sat in the principal's office, Mother explained to the woman that I spoke little English, though that was no longer true and in fact my English was better than Mother's; that my education had been badly disrupted by the war in Europe; and that she had led me out of Soviet-occupied eastern Poland in an eleven-hour trek through the snow, over the Carpathian Mountains, into Hungary; and that a book by her would be out shortly, under the title *Flight to Freedom*.

The principal took careful notes, was duly impressed, and led us to meet the fourth grade teacher and her class in the music room. The teacher's name was Miss Boyd, and her class, consisting of some ten girls and two boys, were singing "Drink to me only with thine eyes, and I will pledge with mine."

As with the British anthem, I knew the meaning of most of the words. One that did give me trouble was *pledge*, and, once more, I put my mind to deducing its meaning. To *drink* to another person with your *eyes* must certainly require some action of the eyelashes, possibly a coquettish fluttering or eyeball rolling, and the only possible response with the other person's eyes had to be something similar. So if *drink* meant something like fluttering the eyelashes, then *pledge* might mean to roll the eyes, or the other way around. And so I came to envision two lovers fluttering or *pledging* their eyelashes at each other across a crowded room. This was a perfectly reasonable image based on what I had seen in the behavior of the older boys and girls in camp on many occasions.

Then Miss Boyd suggested that the following morning I come at eight o'clock so that I could be with my new classmates when they began the school day by "*pledging* to the flag." This suggested an expression of patriotism that I had never seen performed in any other country.

Much to my surprise, I had little difficulty getting along with my new classmates. Most of them were girls, and they were not only respectful of my ignorance of things American, they self-appointed themselves as my interpreters and instructors. There was little I could do during recess, which we took in the park along the Hudson across the street from our school, that I did not have two or more female interpreters at my elbow. During sessions in the school's gymnasium, there was frequently a discussion among the girls as to which apparatus I was to patronize next.

In addition, they were all very interested in hearing the story of my escape from Poland. I took this as an opportunity to right the travesty my mother had made of our adventure by keeping to the unadulterated truth in every detail. I told them about the guide Mother had hired abandoning us and the two of us climbing to the border at the top of the mountain, and then wandering through the woods till we stumbled into a Hungarian village in the middle of the night. Miss Boyd and my classmates listened to my story and expressed admiration for both me and my mother.

In return, I learned about America. America, Miss Boyd told us, was a land of freedom and equality. Everyone in America was equal. And while racial and religious prejudice did exist on the part of certain ignorant individuals and all southerners, it was not the American way. When we put on some kind of pageant at Thanksgiving time, I got a speaking part, even though I was only an immigrant. I was told to write my own speech, which I worked on for two days. What I came up with was, "I am glad to be in a country that has liberty and equality."

There was just one negative note to this school experience. One day Miss Boyd put the letters *G.L.C.* in a corner of the chalkboard, said that they were not to be erased, and explained that they stood for *Good Living Club*, which our entire class comprised.

One day, when another class joined us for some activity, one of the visitors asked me what the letters stood for. I told her and heard a gasp from the girl sitting in front of me. When our visitors had left, this girl raised her hand and then told Miss Boyd that Julian had told a girl from the other class what *G.L.C.* stood for.

There were more gasps from my classmates, and I realized I had done something terrible.

"Julian, didn't you remember my saying that this was to be our secret?" Miss Boyd asked me.

I had absolutely no such memory. And the fact that I could blot something like that right out of my mind would bother me for many years to come.

The next few months were among the happiest of my young life. The solicitous attention I received in school was now echoed in my home life. I would begin the day with eggs that my mother scrambled for me. She would do this in her bathrobe with a kerchief over her hair and night cream on her face in place of the usual makeup. In this state, Mother seemed sincere and vulnerable, a condition she would rarely portray later in the day. She would tell me to be careful crossing the street, give me a dime for ice cream, and hug me goodbye. For the first time in my life, I felt almost like a regular kid.

The one chink in this positive self-image was my name, *Julian*. In Polish it was pronounced "Yulian," and I had known one other Yulian, the well-known Polish poet Yulian Tuwim, to whom I had been introduced in Brazil. I had no objection to the Polish pronunciation of my name, but the only actual *Julian* I had ever met was the awkward, plump, lumpy-nosed boy whom I frequently encountered accidentally in mirrors before looking away quickly and whose greatest expectations tended to be shattered. I wanted no part of that image and envied my two male classmates, John and James, for their single-syllable monikers.

Another reason this time was special was that I knew that the ship to Palestine had finally sailed out of my life. While we were in Hungary, my creative mother felt that I needed to be disciplined and had devised a story about a ship in the harbor that was picking up all Jewish children and taking them to safety in Palestine. She would, she told me, place me on that ship, and I would never see her again, but I would be with all the other Jewish children.

The thought of being separated from Mother and placed in a throng of strange Jewish children was so emotionally wrenching to me at that time that I cried and begged her to reconsider, promising to be good forever. In view of my promise Mother relented, but that ship-in-the-harbor would reappear many times throughout our westward trek—even when there was no harbor.

I soon realized that the ship did not exist, but the idea that my mother would use so twisted and painful a weapon against me was as excruciating as an actual ship, and I would climb all over Mother with kisses and hugs and entreaties to remove the image. Now that we were in America, I was sure Mother would not resort to the device again.

When I returned from school, Mother would usually be there with another hug and a cream cheese and jelly sandwich. For dinner, we would go next door to my aunt and uncle's, since Mother's cooking abilities stopped at scrambled eggs.

There was a parade on Armistice Day, November 11. Marching bands played and soldiers with flags and rifles marched down Broadway, or maybe it was West End Avenue. Gray-haired veterans of the Last War in their puttees and Boy Scout hats marched just as smartly behind them, carrying their own flags. Then, in two or three long, open cars rode some very old men with very white hair and beards. They were dressed in blue or gray uniforms with gold braid and medals and wore wide-brimmed cowboy hats. Judging by their blue uniforms, I assumed those to be retired policemen. Who the two or three old men in gray uniforms might be, I had no idea. I hadn't yet heard of the Civil War.

What wouldn't occur to me till years later was the fact that some of those Civil War veterans that I saw that day must have laid eyes on General Robert E. Lee. General Lee's father, "Lighthorse Harry," was a close friend of George Washington's. This means that I am only three degrees removed from the father of my adopted country.

One evening, Mother and I went for dinner to the Automat. There were a number of Horn & Hardart Automats around town, glass-fronted restaurants inside of which one could see a gleaming wall of little mailbox-like compartments containing a wide variety of meal elements. There were shrimp cocktails, salads, soups, meat, side dishes of vegetables, bread and butter, sandwiches, pies, ice cream, all visible behind their individual little glass-and-chrome doors. There wasn't a waiter or waitress, except those clearing the tables; the customers served themselves by inserting coins into slots and watching the shiny little doors pop open. It was a magic, futuristic world, and whenever I passed one of these restaurants on the street, I would press my face against its glass front and fantasize myself on the inside, procuring a ham sandwich or a slice of apple pie through the process of automation.

On this particular evening, it appeared that the Szyks were entertaining some people that Mother particularly did not want to meet or maybe whom the Szyks didn't want meeting my mother and me. I don't know what the issue was, and I didn't pursue it once I learned that we'd be eating at the Automat.

As she watched me pack away the turkey so that I could return to the chrome cornucopia for a dish of spaghetti, there was a look of satisfaction on Mother's face that I hadn't seen since leaving Brazil. It reminded me of dinners we had eaten there with Sr. Ernesto, the man who had proposed marriage and whom Mother had come close to accepting. I paused long enough to ask whether we would be seeing the *senhor* ever again.

"You liked Ernesto, didn't you?" Mother said.

I told her that I did, but it was *her* affection for him that was foremost in my mind. Looking at Mother's face now, I saw a wistful, vulnerable look that I had never seen there before and would never see again. I had a strange urge to reach out and touch her.

That December, just weeks before our first American Christmas, we heard on the radio that Japan had attacked Pearl Harbor.

"Where is Pearl Harbor?" Mother asked me. It was a Sunday, and Mother was still in her pink bathrobe, though she had wiped the night cream from her face hours earlier. I shrugged my shoulders. Ordinarily Mother would have scolded me for the discourtesy, but this time she had other things on her mind. "Doesn't your teacher tell you about geography?" she said.

I said that, to my knowledge, she didn't. We rushed upstairs to my aunt and uncle's for information. Uncle Arthur would tell us where Pearl Harbor was. Opening her terrace doors to us, Aunt Julia acknowledged that she didn't know either, and Uncle Arthur was on the telephone with an editor.

When his phone call was finished, Uncle Arthur told us about a commission he had just received for a series of caricatures featuring Japanese warmongers. Then he explained where Pearl Harbor was and the strategic significance of the raid. As we sat around the radio listening for further news, Mother and Uncle Arthur exchanged occasional, knowing looks. America had entered the war.

Chapter Three

As school broke for the Christmas vacation, Mother informed me that I would not be returning for the winter term. Instead, I would be going to a boarding school in Connecticut. Incredibly, the rusty old ship to Palestine had chugged up the Hudson River.

When I asked why the lifestyle that seemed to be working so well for the first time needed to be altered, Mother told me that all upper-class boys in England went to boarding schools. We much admired England in those war years, and, if that was the case, then I had little argument to use against her plan. Anita and Andy, she said, were attending boarding school, and I realized that their companionship would certainly soften the harsh-sounding experience.

In preparation for my new life and armed with a list supplied by this new school, Mother took me to the boys' department at Saks Fifth Avenue where I was fitted for a tweed suit with knee-length knickerbockers, a gray suit with both knickerbockers and short pants, and a navy blue suit with long pants only. The long-panted blue suit, the two white shirts, and the black shoes were to be worn only on Sundays, at which time they were mandatory. Then we bought tan shirts, ties, and brown shoes for weekday use.

Then on a certain day I put on the new tweed suit with the knickerbockers and we packed the rest into one

of Mother's suitcases, along with the other things specified
on the list, and headed for Grand Central Terminal. As
our taxi turned the corner onto Park Avenue and I could
see the terminal building plugging the thoroughfare several
blocks ahead, I felt the way I imagined a condemned man
feels upon first seeing the electric chair. Only reminding
myself of the promised company of Anita and Andy quieted
my anxiety somewhat.

A man on the train platform with the words *Rumsey
Hall*, the name of my new school, lettered on a piece of
paper pinned to his lapel and holding a clipboard introduced himself as master on duty. He checked off my name
and directed us into the car that my new schoolmates were
occupying. Mother explained to him that I didn't speak
much English since we had only recently escaped from
Soviet-occupied Poland by crossing the Carpathian Mountains on foot—an exploit soon to be chronicled in her
book. He, in turn, assured her that I would be well taken
care of and urged that we find a seat for me and say our
good-byes.

Holding a new comic book in my free hand, I dragged
my suitcase down the car's aisle, scanning left and right
for signs of my two cousins. I did not see them. In fact,
there were no girls at all among my new schoolmates, and
I wondered if Anita and Andy might be in a different,
co-ed car.

"Why don't you sit here, next to this boy," Mother
said in Polish, indicating an empty seat. "He looks nice.
Introduce yourself, look him in the eye, and shake his
hand firmly."

Ordinarily I would have taken umbrage at being
instructed to do what I had been trained to do by Kiki
years ago, but I didn't want our parting to be on a hostile

note. "How do you do? My name is Julian Padowicz," I said, holding out my hand.

The boy looked older than me. His face was covered with the pimples that I had found to be a sign of adolescence. He turned his head to glance at me, then buried it again in the comic book he was reading. I noticed that it was a *Captain America* comic that I hadn't yet read, which was good. At camp I had learned the practice of exchanging finished comic books.

"Well, sit down anyway," Mother said, again in Polish.

At that moment the master on duty showed up beside us and hefted my suitcase onto the overhead rack. "Brewer, shake hands with Padowicz," he instructed the boy in the seat, at which point the boy held out a limp hand, his eyes still in his comic book. As we shook hands, the master smiled at Mother and assured her that I would get along just fine.

As Mother and I parted, she whispered in my ear, still in Polish, "Tell everyone that you're Catholic. There will be someone to take you to church every Sunday. And also tell them about my book."

With the train moving slowly under New York streets, the master who had first greeted us came walking along the aisle checking off names again. Reaching my seat, he stopped to make sure I was all right. I assured him that I was. Then I asked about the whereabouts of my two cousins. There were no girls at Rumsey, he informed me, and there was no Andrew Potok on the school rolls. If Anita and Andy indeed attended boarding school, as Mother had told me, I now realized it wasn't Rumsey Hall.

We had just come out of the tunnel and were on an elevated track, where you could look into the lighted windows of apartment houses, and my eyes were attracted to them as they rushed by. I saw dark-skinned people sitting or moving in some of those windows and realized that lives were being lived in those buildings—people were talking to each other, mothers cooking supper, waiting for their husbands to return from work. Boys like me were doing their homework as I had done a few weeks before, but knowing that, in a while, the family would be assembled around the dinner table—while I, I suddenly realized, was rushing to a place where I knew no one, sitting now beside a boy who didn't want to talk to me, and I had been fooled into believing that I would have Anita and Andy for support.

But why should I be surprised? I had the feeling that I was being transported into an alien testosterone world where unknown crises awaited me.

Rumsey Hall consisted of several large wooden buildings in Cornwall Village. The village was a group of single-family homes along several streets, and you could walk from one end to the other in half an hour. There was a public library, a Protestant church, a post office with a candy counter, and a telephone switchboard operated by a woman and her daughter in their home. Whenever the operator said "Number please," it was one of these two ladies. The rest was all residential, except for Rumsey.

The school's main building was Greek Revival in style, with a colonnade and wide wooden stairs facing the street. The dormitory, dining hall, common room, and office were all housed within. The bathroom was in the basement. Some thirty yards behind stood the wooden school building with a study hall on the first floor and classrooms upstairs. A gymnasium with the definite look of a converted barn stood behind the school building. Off to the side stood the little house that was the infirmary and, beyond it, the residence of one of the masters and his wife with a section in which most of the senior class were housed, called the annex. When I became a senior and came to live in the annex, I would learn through bitter experience that it had no heat and, probably, no insulation.

My first roommate was a boy named Peter Snapper, a third former with a brush cut. I was to be assigned to the second form, equating with fourth grade. There were maybe seven of us in the second form and forty-some students in the entire school. Explaining the situation to me that first night, speaking in a whisper which I could hear in my upper bunk but presumably the prefect patrolling the hall could not, Snapper explained to me that the sixth formers were called *seniors* and one of them was patrolling our hall at that very moment. Seniors were endowed with special powers. Some of them served as prefects, each in charge of a portion of the living quarters and making sure that the boys under his authority kept their rooms neat, turned out their lights at a certain time, and didn't talk or leave their beds after lights-out. And whether they were prefects or not, *all* seniors had the authority to report boys for various rule violations.

Suddenly I felt my chest tense up as I imagined one of the older boys I had seen that evening walking up and down our hall with a report pad and a pencil at the ready. Back in occupied Poland, Russian soldiers had patrolled the streets ready to enforce the occupation with their guns. At the French school, before the war, older boys took pleasure in appearing at our recess to trip us as we ran by, for no reason at all, or push us to the ground. Two brothers on the ship to Brazil had tried to push me overboard. A group of boys had tried to rob me during *Carnival* in Brazil. I had firsthand experience with cruelty and treachery from other boys, but my ability to fight back and to run had enabled me to survive. But a report to authority was something you couldn't fight or run from. Eventually, it would find its way to the commissar, and the weight of the entire government would be aligned against you. The idea of report powers in the hands of fourteen-year-olds was a frightening thing.

Surely this feature could not have been explained to Mother in the literature describing Rumsey Hall. She couldn't know that, at this very moment, there was a boy only four years older than me out in the hall ready to report me for whispering or being whispered to. She couldn't know that, at this moment, I was curled up in the under-brush of a predatory jungle trying to keep my whimpers from being heard.

"Padowicz, are you asleep?" my roommate whispered. I thought it best to pretend that I was. Then the door opened. "Stop the talking," a figure said from the doorway.

"We're not talking," Snapper answered. "The jerk is crying."

Sometime during that first term my whimpering stopped, and by the time we went home for spring vacation I had no idea what it had all been about. But the moment that vacation and several more ended and new terms started, my homesickness began again and lasted well into the middle of the term. And the taxi ride along Park Avenue with Grand Central looming ahead at the end of each vacation had the emotional impact of walking the last mile.

The way that this report system worked was that misbehavior, tardiness, or dress-code violations were dealt with at a session called *Announcements*, which followed rest period after lunch every weekday. For this session, we would all sit at our desks in the study hall while Mr. Sherry, the owner/director, or Mr. Barr, the headmaster, sat at the large desk on the raised platform in front of the hall in the role of judge and dealt with the accumulated reports. He would pick up a piece of folded paper, read it silently while expressing a series of emotions with his face, and finally read out a name.

"Padowicz, I have a report here that you were a minute and a half tardy for breakfast this morning. Is that true?" The expression on his face as he read the report would often be one of incredulity, as though actually hoping for a denial.

You would have risen to your feet by that time, and you would answer courageously, "Yes, sir, it is."

"I am sorry to hear that, Padowicz. Punctuality is a virtue, you know. Do you know what the word *virtue* means?"

"I think so, sir."

"You only *think* so? I would like you to *know* the meaning of virtue. Why don't you look up the definition in your dictionary and write it out for me by Announcements tomorrow."

"Yes, sir," you would say and begin to sit down.

"Just a moment, Padowicz," the judge would say. "We haven't finished yet. We have to deal with this tardiness, don't we?"

"Yes, sir."

"So you say that you were indeed tardy, as specified."

"Yes, sir."

"Was there a reason for this tardiness, Padowicz?"

"I couldn't find my shoe," you would say, under your breath.

"We can't hear you, Padowicz. Could you speak up a little more? Your schoolmates are all interested."

"I couldn't find my shoe, sir."

"You couldn't find your shoe. Now that is a very valid reason. You can't very well show up at breakfast with just one shoe, can you?"

There would be a titter through the study hall, and you would see a slight glimmer of hope that your plight would be given legitimacy.

"This is a very serious matter," the judge would admonish the titterers. "A gentleman does not appear at breakfast with just one shoe. Was that the right shoe or the left shoe, Padowicz?"

"It was my left shoe, sir." At this point you would get the feeling that you were being trifled with.

"Well, that certainly is a very good reason to be tardy for breakfast, don't you agree?"

"Yes, sir," you would say, knowing full well that it could not save you from what awaited.

"But it isn't an excuse," the judge would declare. "It's a valid reason, but it is not an excuse. Three marks!"

Three marks against your name was not usually a big deal, as long as they were the only marks you received that week. Marks were counted against your team, the Reds or the Blues. I was assigned to the Blues on my first day at Rumsey, and remained a Blue for the rest of my Rumsey experience. At the end of the week, the marks were tallied up and the team with the least received some small privilege. If I remember correctly, it was taking the Wednesday afternoon study hall in your room, but I may be wrong. At the end of the term, however, the team with the least marks would be taken to the movies in Torrington while the losers had to do cleanup around the campus.

Each team had a set of officers, elected at the start of each term, and these officers would determine the punishments that would be doled out for excessive mark accumulations. The teams would meet in their designated meeting rooms every Tuesday, read off each member's accumulated marks for the week, and impose the punishments according to the rules set up by these officers.

A popular (among the enforcers) punishment involved the Saturday evening movie. Each Saturday, after supper, a movie would be shown in the gymnasium with frequent pauses for reel changing by the sixth-former projectionist, as well as for correcting flagrant synchronization issues between picture and sound, speaker cords disconnected by shuffling feet, and other malfunctions.

So many marks accumulated, and you had to miss the first half hour of the film. So many more marks, and you missed the first hour. And for so many marks, you got to miss the movie altogether. It was in my second year, I believe, that some creative team enforcer came up with an even better movie punishment. That was to make you sit under the screen, where you heard the sound track blaring in your ear from the speaker, but could not see the picture.

There were other forms of punishment that involved paddling, often accompanied by considerable crying, that were tried—sometimes adopted and sometimes abandoned, depending on how well they worked to control the accumulation of marks. One six-year-old boy, who in my opinion belonged in boarding school even less than I did, was constantly compiling marks for our team by appearing with an improperly tied tie or his shirt not fully tucked in. His howls, as he was paddled for his transgressions, brought tears to my eyes.

For me, these Saturday movies—stories involving mothers, fathers, wives, sweethearts, pets, and supportive siblings—were what I waited for all week. For the two-plus hours (including changing reels and projector repairs) of the showing I would live in a world where the good and just were eventually appreciated, even though posthumously at times, where dreams came true, and reason prevailed. Then I would emerge with a splitting headache, make my way gingerly back toward the main building, and sometimes throw up behind the bicycle shed. The nurse attributed this to eye strain, but years later my doctor would tell me that migraine could be brought about by the release of tension.

Chapter Four

On the academic front it was quickly discovered, to no one's great surprise, that I wasn't reading up to grade level. Unfamiliarity with the language was one reason. Another was that, except for the little reading I had done with Kiki before starting school in Warsaw, this was the first time that I knew enough of a language to be expected to actually read it. And so at the age of ten, for all intents and purposes I was learning a skill that others acquired with the flexibility of six- and seven-year-old minds.

During a certain study hall period every day I would go back to the main building and up the stairs to Headmaster Barr's apartment where his wife, an elderly lady in a wheelchair, tutored me in reading. She would hold the book and move her knobby finger along the page while I sounded out the words. As more English words were added to my vocabulary, my reading aloud improved. I even reached the point at which I could give dramatic inflection to what I read, and my tutor praised this as real progress. By the end of the year, she proclaimed that my reading was up to grade level.

But then why did I have such difficulty finishing the reading assignments handed out by my classroom teachers? Why was it that when a teacher instructed us to read a passage silently in class before continuing the discussion and then said, "All right, you should all be finished by now," I was only halfway through it? And then, when the master asked me questions pertaining to that text, I couldn't answer him, even for the half that I had read. "I'm s . . . sorry, Mr. T . . . Tisdale," I would explain, "I didn't finish r . . . reading it." At times of stress, my stammering would return.

"Did anyone else have trouble finishing it?" Mr. Tisdale would ask, and heads would shake.

"Then let's read it again, together, Padowicz. Read it aloud for us."

I would read the entire passage aloud, and Mr. Tisdale would say that my reading was very good, and that I must not have been paying attention the first time. But as he went on to quiz us, we would often discover, much to my embarrassment and the amusement of my classmates, that even after having reread the material aloud and being praised for the reading, I still had little idea of what the passage contained.

Following a hunch, I conducted an experiment of my own in evening study hall. I selected a passage in my history book and timed myself reading the passage on the big clock ticking at the front of the room. Then, mouthing the words so nobody would hear me, I timed myself rereading the passage "aloud." Just as I had suspected, it turned out that I read silently at exactly the same speed as I read aloud. I knew that this wasn't as it was supposed to be. Silent reading, where you were supposed to just recognize the words without the burden of enunciating them, was supposed to be considerably faster than reading aloud. But I discovered now that when I was supposed to just recognize words I was still enunciating them in my mind. I was impressed with my deduction but perplexed by my reading problem. When I tried to just recognize words, it didn't work unless I enunciated them in my mind.

I tried to teach myself to recognize words without enunciating them, but it just wouldn't work. I put it down to the problem of reading in a second language. Unfortunately, I had no Polish reading material to test the theory fully.

But what this still did not explain was why, after my teacher had given me the time to read the entire passage in class and I had read every word aloud, I still had not known much of what was in it. How was it that my eyes had seen and my mouth had enunciated each word, but my mind hadn't been listening? "Padowicz, didn't you just finish reading the passage?" my disappointed teacher would ask. I would confirm that I had. "Then how come you have no idea what it said?" I had no answer.

The problem became even more clearly defined on Saturdays, when we had spelling tests. Again the second language theory seemed to explain my poor performance on these tests. But when I had been sent downstairs to my desk in the study hall to write each misspelled word correctly one hundred times and then immediately returned to class for a retest, I found myself misspelling them again—and not necessarily with the same errors as before. Once more, I realized, I had an incidence of my mind not being present when my eyes and my hand were performing their assigned task.

How this could be I could not understand. Had I shared this observation with one of the masters, I knew very well what he would have said: "Padowicz, you are clearly not paying attention." And not paying attention was a cardinal sin here at Rumsey, as it had been at the Riverside school and even the Brazilian school in Rio. (I have no idea what the cardinal sin had been at the French school.) Not pay-

ing attention was a common offense of those schoolboys
who weren't interested in learning, in being good students
and good people. I did not want to be a bad person, but,
apparently, there was a fault in my character that would
eventually compel me to become exactly that. It was something like my Uncle Benek who had gone crazy while
attending university.

Mother came to visit me one Sunday. She had originally
promised to come the Sunday before, and I had sat on
the wide, wooden front steps of our main building waiting for her arrival with Rod, my new roommate, whom
at Mother's suggestion I had invited to come and have
lunch with us. When one of the masters discovered us
sitting there, I explained that my mother was coming to
take us to lunch.

It was around three when someone came out of the
office to tell me that Western Union was on the phone
for me. It was a telegram from Mother saying she couldn't
make it but would be there the following Sunday. Why
she hadn't telephoned me directly to tell me so herself I
didn't understand.

This time she did show up, with a gray-haired Mr. David,
who drove a black Cadillac convertible and kept looking
at his watch. They brought me a box of chocolates, and I
showed them my room and the school building. Mother
seemed to have forgotten the promise of lunch and for the
second Sunday in a row I went without a noonday meal.

When they were ready to leave, I was gripped by a
terrible anticipation of renewed homesickness and begged
Mother in Polish to take me home from this hateful place.
Mother smiled and told me, in English, that I should smile
as well. People only liked people who smiled, she said, at
which point Mr. David broke into a grin. Switching at

last to Polish she said, the smile still on her face, "Oh my god, how you embarrass me with your constant long face."

One day in history class the master said we were going to have a treat. Instead of the scheduled discussion of the way of life in colonial America, "Padowicz is going to tell us about his exciting escape from occupied Poland." I had had no prior warning about this, but I wasn't concerned since I had been put in this same situation at my prior school in New York. The master, Mr. Gregg, I realized, was the same one who had shepherded us on the train from Grand Central that first time and whom Mother had told about our escape. And I also strongly suspected that he had not prepared properly for a discussion on colonial life.

I enjoyed standing up in front of the class and proceeded to tell about how Mother and I disguised ourselves as peasants by turning our clothes inside out and rode in a horse-drawn sleigh to the foot of the mountain on the top of which was the Hungarian border. I explained how our hired guide told the Soviet officer at the guard shack, who knew him from his traveling back and forth, that he was taking my mother and me to his village where he and my mother were going to marry. Then we had driven along the foot of the mountain until the guard walking along the road in front of us and the one behind us were both facing away from us. At that moment the sleigh was to stop, my mother, I, and the guide were to jump out, and the guide was to carry me on his back to the top of the mountain while his nephew continued on to their village with the sleigh. Then our guide was supposed to lead us on foot to a nearby Hungarian village.

But what really happened, I explained, was that when my mother and I jumped out of the sleigh, our guide didn't—he just drove off with his nephew, leaving us to cope on our own. We climbed the mountain by ourselves, then wandered for eleven hours in the woods till we stumbled into the Hungarian village in the middle of the night.

Then, when we thought our escape was complete, the Hungarian border authorities wanted to send us back to the Bolsheviks in Poland.

As I described this in detail, telling about the cold and the fact that our sandwiches froze so we couldn't eat them and being dead tired and frightened, I could see the intense interest on the part of my classmates.

But then Mr. Gregg interrupted me, "I think that's enough Padowicz. You've demonstrated that you have a vivid imagination and in English class it should stand you in good stead. But this is a history class, and I thought you would give us a taste of what it's like in Europe right now. But you've taken my trust in you as an opportunity to exercise your creativity and aggrandize your ego at the expense of my faith. Please sit down." I did not try to tell my story again.

Rumsey issued report cards every week. It was placed in your mailbox and you received two grades. One was a numerical average of the grading you had received on homework and tests during that week for each subject. The other was an effort grade, reflecting the effort that you were judged to be applying. You either made the Effort List or you didn't, and a negative vote from a single master, a single incomplete homework paper, would automatically keep you off that list. Doing your homework in your room instead of in study hall was the reward that fifth and sixth formers were given for making this Effort List. For second formers like me, the fact that you were judged to have made the appropriate effort was supposed to be enough. I think about a third of the students made it every week.

That I made the list several times during the winter term, my first at Rumsey, was nice, but I had bigger problems to contend with. Unless I could find a solution to my reading problems, other people's recognition of my efforts was nothing for me to concern myself with.

It was during the spring term that I made some quantitative discoveries regarding my errant mind. It seemed, I realized, that my mind was constantly whirling, whether I was reading or listening or walking to class. It was constantly playing little movies, scenes of stories I had read or heard or just made up. The Three Musketeers were clashing swords with the cardinal's men, or the retired boxer from the film *How Green Was My Valley* was manhandling the mean schoolteacher, or some purely imagined boy was bringing a rabbit he had shot to his mother for that evening's dinner and she was telling him how proud she was of him.

And when I was reading something while this was going on, I of course had no idea what I was reading except that something I read might deflect the movie in my mind in an even newer direction. A math problem regarding a farmer's herd of cows might cause the mother in my internal movie to ask her son to go find the missing milk cow and send him off on a new adventure. But the problem my textbook was trying to pose would not register without my rereading the problem several times and forcing its content past my fictional characters.

Or I might be reading in my history book about Ethan Allen marching his men through the woods and assimilating that because it interested me, until the account of them wading across a river sent the image of Huckleberry Finn floating down the Mississippi with an escaped Negro slave from last Saturday's movie across my mind. Then I would try to feel what it must have been like to be a slave, and my heart would ache for the little black children being sold away from their parents. By the time I realized that this had nothing to do with what Ethan Allen's men were doing, they had already reached Fort Ticonderoga and were laying siege to it. How they had gotten from chest deep in the river to Fort Ticonderoga in dry uniforms I had no idea, except that, according to page numbers, there were four pages that I had read but could not account for.

This certainly explained my study difficulties. While I was reading and turning pages, my mind was off on its own trip through the woods. It was like a horse who, instead of following the trail, had taken off on its own. Except that I could not make that horse follow that trail. I could bring him back to the trail by pulling hard on the reins, which also stopped him, but the moment I loosened the reins for him to proceed he would veer off again on his own. My own brain was that unruly, undirectable, and therefore useless horse.

If this wasn't a definition of going crazy, like my Uncle Ben, I didn't know what was. But, once more, why should I be surprised by this happening to me? While I dared not share this finding for the consequences that would follow, I knew that there was really little point in my learning multiplication tables or historical facts since they would be of little use to a crazy man in the future.

When realizations like this hit or when something reminded me of home with Mother and my homesickness returned, I would count the days until Saturday evening when the lights would dim, Rumsey would drop away, and I would become a member of a complete family—or one that, by the end of the movie, would have become a complete family.

Some time before the start of summer vacation, I was called into the housemother's work room. Her name was Mrs. Smith, and she was a nice lady who seemed to sense my adjustment problems and would call me in occasionally to give me a cookie. The other guys made fun of the plump, curly-haired, middle-aged Mrs. Smith, but I liked her. This time she said that there was a package for me. All packages had to be opened in Mrs. Smith's presence and some items, such as boxes of cookies, retained in her work room for gradual distribution to the addressee.

Unwrapping the package, I saw a book in a blue jacket. "*Flight to Freedom* by Barbara Padowicz," it said. It showed two small figures trudging through deep snow. One of those unrecognizable figures, I knew, was me. On the back there was a portrait of my mother.

"Oh, your mother's written a book," Mrs. Smith said, reading Mother's name over my shoulder. "Isn't she beautiful!"

I agreed that Mother was, indeed, beautiful and handed the book to Mrs. Smith so she could take a closer look at the photograph. In a moment she had opened the cover. "Oh, and look, there's an inscription to you," she said. "It must be in Polish, but I can see the name *Julian*."

I read the inscription. "To my dear Yulian," it said, "Make sure you show this to everyone in school. Love, Mother."

Suddenly, as I absorbed Mother's message to me, I was aware of a great disparity between my mother and myself. While I was sure that in my place Mother would have certainly found a way for everyone in school to learn about the existence of the book and of our dramatic story, just as she had found a way to get her book written in English and published, there was no way in the world that I could accomplish what she was asking of me. I knew that it was important. I knew that every copy that sold paid a certain portion of that sale price to Mother, and that the money was essential to us. But to jump up suddenly at lunch or morning roll call and shout, "Look everybody, my mother's written a book!" was something I just would not be able to do. There were a great many things that my mother could do for which I just did not have the capacity.

For Mrs. Smith I translated the inscription as, "Let us never forget our adventure together." Then I took the book to study hall and, hiding it behind one of my textbooks, proceeded to read it myself.

There were a lot of exciting things in the book, some that were true and some that weren't. I was used, by then, to Mother's downplaying my contributions in order to make herself look more heroic. After all, this was her book. What did surprise me, however, was the fact that much of what had involved me had been totally left out. Incidents that did not make me any kind of hero had either been left out or written in such a way that my presence wasn't even noted. There had been incidents, such as our scene with Hungarian border security or Mother getting her leg caught under the frozen log, where my actions had clearly affected the outcome, but here they were presented in such a way that I was no more than a spectator. I couldn't help being disappointed.

I received a surprise telephone call from Mother one evening. Mother did not normally call me but, I suspect, something had come up in her day that had awakened some sentiment toward me. She had nothing special to tell me but simply wanted to ask how things were going.

For my part, I considered this a most fortunate coincidence since the day before I had received a great gift from the coach of our lower-school baseball team. Mr. Mulligan had told us about a domain I had never heard of before,

called *good sportsmanship*. What made the concept so pre-
cious to me was the fact that, according to Mr. Mulligan,
winning was not the be-all and end-all of sports, and that
how you played the game was far more important. Winning, except in informal foot races, was not something I was
much used to in life, and the idea that one could actually
receive approval and esteem by exhibiting genuine effort
and respect for one's opponents, something I definitely
could do, promised to be a life changer for me.

I had, in fact, written some lines translating the concept into Polish for inclusion in the following Sunday's
compulsory letter home, but Mother's surprise phone call
had made it possible for me to share my excitement more
directly with her. But instead of sharing in my newfound
enthusiasm, Mother proceeded to shred it by telling me
how absolutely wrong my coach had been and that winning
was, indeed, the only thing of importance. If you lost, she
said, nobody cared how you played the game or how hard
you tried. And as for respecting your opponent, that was
a practice of losers and a sure formula for failure.

I did not argue the issue with her, as I had well learned
not to, but I was again very much aware of my mother
and me moving along diverging paths. I would not let go
of Mr. Mulligan's gospel but rather realized again that in
some areas Mother was wrong and I was right—though it
would often cost me.

When I arrived at Grand Central for the start of summer
vacation, Mother met me with the words, "Did everybody
see my book?" Keeping my eyes on the concrete of the
platform, I assured her that *most* of the people had.

Her next words were to tell me that that evening we
would be eating at a Chinese restaurant as guests of a very

wealthy man named Reggie, who wanted to marry her. And that I should be sure to smile and act happy.

Mother's instruction to smile functioned like a mantra, taking me back to her visit months before when I had cried to be taken home and been told that I should smile instead. There was something terribly pathetic about the little boy I had been that afternoon, and it was a moment I didn't enjoy revisiting.

"Are you cold?" Mother asked.

I said that I wasn't.

"But you shuddered."

"I don't think so."

"You did."

But this marriage business was news indeed. Not that Mother hadn't received other proposals of marriage during our journey from Warsaw. Even Colonel Bawatchov, occupational commander of Durnoval, had proposed to Mother before our escape and promised to personally teach her to drive a tractor. But, with the exception of Sr. Ernesto in Brazil, Mother had referred to them all later with a laugh or a sarcastic remark. That she should endow this suitor's intentions with such respect I considered a milestone. From my own perspective, the idea of a father figure and the possibility of a home to which I could return from school every afternoon was very welcome.

I had never been to a Chinese restaurant, and this one was on the second floor overlooking Times Square. To my great dismay, our host was a very large and very old man with a bald head and ample jowls hanging down around his chin. His name was Reginald Purbrick, and he spoke in a loud voice with a heavy British accent.

Mr. Purbrick sat at the head of a long table with Mother on his right, me at the other end, and three other couples between us. "It's the best Chinese food in New York," he announced in a voice that implied that he knew such things.

"What is the title of your mother's book again?" the lady on my right whispered.

"It's *Flight to Freedom*," I whispered back.

"Oh yes, *Flight to Freedom*," she repeated quietly. Then, aloud, "I just read your book, Mrs. Padarewski. It's so thrilling." Changing our name, Padowicz, to Padarewski was a common occurrence. Ignatius Padarewski, a fellow Pole, was a well-known concert pianist and Polish statesman at the time.

"She is a veritable heroine," Mr. Purbrick proclaimed. "A veritable heroine."

A year and a half earlier, I would have bristled at the fact that my heroism wasn't acknowledged as well, but I knew better now. At the other end of the table, Mother smiled and put her delicate hand on top of Purbrick's baseball mitt of a paw.

Later that evening, as his chauffeur held open the car door in front of our apartment building, Purbrick said, "Barbara, I have to fly back to England tomorrow."

"So soon?" Mother said.

"I'm afraid so."

"Then let me put Julian to bed, and I'll be right down," Mother said. "Wait for me."

My bed was the same sofa I had slept on before, and as Mother proceeded to make it up with sheets and a blanket, something that I had had to do for myself before, she explained that Reggie was a Member of Parliament and a personal friend of Winston Churchill's who travelled between London and New York on government business.

Then, asking if I was sure I didn't mind being left alone—a question she had not asked in strange hotel rooms in Budapest or Dubrovnik or Rome or Barcelona or Lisbon or Rio when I had been eight and terrified—and instructing me to lock the door behind her, Mother hurried out of the apartment.

I remembered the night terrors I had endured in the Budapest hotel room when the doily that mother had draped over the lamp created threatening shadows on the walls. But I was beyond that now. Witches and goblins were something that I realized I had outgrown. I had other terrors.

Chapter Five

Two days later, I was back at camp with Anita and Andy. But this was a different camp than the summer before. This one was on Long Island on the campus of the Hudson School, the boarding school that my two cousins did, indeed, attend. The camp season hadn't yet begun. In fact, that school's spring term hadn't ended but Mother had business to attend to, and arrangements had been made for me to arrive at camp a week or two early.

Every school term ends with final exams, and Hudson School was no exception. Having finished final exams at Rumsey several days earlier, I was just in time to take more final exams here. There was no reason for me to be taking exams here, but I was a ten-year-old of unknown disposition, and letting me loose on the campus for a couple days was risky business. So I was instructed to go wherever my cousin Andy went and do whatever Andy did.

I was not happy about this until I realized that the answers I gave on my exam paper mattered to no one and would probably be read by no one. This, I realized, presented new possibilities. In response to a question regarding reproduction of one-celled animals, to which I well knew the correct answer, I proceeded to write about male cells meeting female cells, taking them to dinner and the movies, and marrying in St. Patrick's Cathedral before going uptown to the hospital to buy a baby cell.

At Rumsey, I had fulfilled writing assignments by writing about American soldiers encountering Japanese soldiers in the jungle and annihilating them, but I had never attempted pure fantasy before. I found I enjoyed it. A question regarding the identity of the father of our country, whom I knew well to be George Washington, I answered by writing about an old Indian still living in the mountains of Arizona who was actually the first human to set foot on American soil. I was sorry when I ran out of paper.

Returning to Rumsey for my second year, I had the sense that reading would no longer present a problem for me. The boy I had been at Hudson Camp that summer was not the same kid who had stuttered and struggled his way through the previous academic year. This summer I had won foot races and swimming races and shown particular skill at archery, to the extent that I was made assistant to the archery instructor. Besides, when the activity lists for the day were posted on the bulletin board, I had had no trouble deciphering them. I really could not visualize the reading assignments at Rumsey giving me any further trouble. I had heard the expression "growing out" of something, and I was sure that I had grown out of my reading problems and, with my stammering issue well under control, could look forward to a life of normalcy. Not only that, but I would work even harder and bequeath to my mother my grades in the nineties and Effort List appearances every week.

But seated at my newly assigned desk in the study hall the evening following our first day of classes, I discovered how wrong I had been. I read the assigned chapter about our bodies "burning oxygen," the heel of one hand forcing the facts into my forehead, and was totally unable to visualize the process they were talking about. If there really was a fire inside my chest, I would surely feel it. But seeing the word *burns* did bring up an image of a house fire, and I wondered how I would get out of my second-floor room if the hallway caught on fire. This led to contemplating a future as a fireman and the sensation of standing on the running board of a speeding, red fire engine. Try as I might to get my sinful mind to follow the words printed in my textbook, I could not do it as I raced around New York on that ladder truck.

Then a piece of the sky fell in. In maybe the fourth week of the term, I got a telephone call from Mother. Apparently, while accompanying me to the train some weeks earlier Mother had met a Mrs. Bradley, mother of Charley Bradley, a fifth former, and learned that Charley made the Effort List almost every week. Up till then she hadn't known what the Effort List was, but Mrs. Bradley had, apparently, gone and explained it. And now Mother was concerned that, according to the report card the school inserted into my letters home, I hadn't made it once since the start of the term.

I explained that the Effort List was very hard to make, to which Mother responded that Mrs. Bradley had not seemed overly intelligent and she doubted that her son was either. So if he could make the Effort List, it was quite disgraceful that I had not.

The sense I got from the conversation was that Mother didn't really understand what the Effort List was all about, and that part was good. I promised that I would try harder and did, in fact, make an extra effort that week to bend my mind to its task. But my mind seemed willing to do very little bending in that direction.

What my mind did seem willing to do was to find faces in the grain of my wooden desktop or the back of the chair of the kid in front of me or sailing ships in the eraser tracks on the chalkboard or African animals in the water stains in the ceiling's acoustic tile—the same way that, two years earlier, it had found witches and goblins in the shadows cast by the doily that Mother had put over the light in our hotel room. But what was particularly damning was that my mind was perfectly willing to go along when the content interested me. For example, I could read stories by O. Henry or Ring Lardner or Jack London and recall every detail, even repeat passages verbatim. But the problems in my math book I had to read four and five times over in order to *sometimes* understand what they were asking. I could read pages in my science or history book till Hell froze over and still have no idea what I had just read.

Then, some weeks later, there was another phone call. "I'm putting Mr. Michael on the phone," Mother said. I knew Mr. Michael from Poland. He was a gray-haired official in the Polish embassy in Washington and an old friend of my mother's who had traveled back and forth between Poland and America before the war. Mr. Michael, I knew, had as a boy been a cadet in the Russian tsar's army.

"Do you know how hard your mother has to work to keep you in that school?" Mr. Michael now said into my ear, in a demanding tone I had not heard him use before.

I admitted that I did not. For that matter, I didn't even know what it was that my mother did.

"Well, shame on you. Your mother works very, very hard so that you can go to Rumsey Hall. And you, instead of being grateful for her efforts, make a mockery of your responsibilities as a son and as a student. Do you have any idea how much it costs her to keep you in that school?"

I was deeply pained by the image of Mother struggling, exhausted, perhaps over some machine, to keep me at Rumsey. "I want to come home," I said.

"You will not come home," Mr. Michael said. "You will remain at that school and you will set your mind to learning your lessons. Do you know what happens to men who do not have the moral fiber to work diligently at their duties?"

The answer to what happens to men who don't have the moral fiber to work diligently did not come readily to my mind, but the question itself made me realize that Mr. Michael had a good grasp of what the Effort List was all about. He went on to explain. "They become drunks and derelicts sleeping in attics and alleys and vomiting all over themselves."

The idea of that becoming my life gripped my heart the way Mother's threat to put me on a ship to Palestine with other Jewish children had done in Budapest. That time, I had been able to make her relent by crying and promising to behave and love her for the rest of my life, but changing this particular reality was beyond Mr. Michael's powers. The only person who could affect that outcome was me, and I understood now that I had not the capacity to do that. I had tried. I had tried very hard, on many occasions, to muster the effort required to fulfill my moral obligations, and I could try no harder. Mr. Michael and my mother didn't know it, but I understood that I wasn't just a boy not applying himself enough, but a bad child who had not the moral fiber to compete in the world. While Mr. Michael's graphic description may have been somewhat exaggerated for my benefit, the fact was that I was destined to become a failure.

I had heard of men who were failures. I didn't know them personally, but I had heard grownups speak of so-and-so or such-and-such being one, and I had a mental picture of a man in at attic room, housed and fed by caring but disappointed relatives as he grew into old age and, finally, passed into the direct hands of God. They didn't, of course, marry or produce unsuccessful children but just waited for their life to end.

Now I had a clear image of the form that my craziness would take. Until then I had only had the image of Uncle Benek, whom I had seen a few times walking around his parents' apartment prattling to himself. Now I could visualize quite clearly the attic to which I would be confined and where meals would be brought to me on a tray.

I wondered whether I would be permitted to complete my schooling, particularly since I had discovered the game of ice hockey and found myself surprisingly competent at it. I wondered whether I would finish school and then prove my ineptitude at some job, or whether my condition would be diagnosed before then and I would be yanked out of school and sent directly to my attic. I wondered what relatives of ours had an attic. Under the circumstances, it was hardly worth making an effort.

It was that very next Friday that Mr. Murray, who had taught us science the year before but now taught us English, assigned us a short story to write over the weekend. In science class last year Mr. Murray would fill class time by having us read aloud from our textbook or he would read to us from an adventure novel. This year, teaching English, he gave out a lot of writing assignments, which we would read aloud once they had been graded while he looked out of the window. My story that week was about a failure waiting in his attic for his nephew to bring him some hot soup.

When we got our papers back on Tuesday, I found mine pockmarked with red pencil, as my papers always were, indicating the many misspellings. My grade, a result of the misspellings, was a forty, twenty points below passing. In the margin, Mr. Murray had written, "When you don't know how to spell a word, don't guess. Look it up in the dictionary."

When I thought that I didn't know how to spell a word, I would certainly look it up. But how was I to know that *women* was not spelled with a *y*, or that *tough* had a *gh* where there should have been an *f*?

This particular morning I was the third to read aloud and discovered, to my great surprise and delight, that my classmates sat engrossed in my story, just as they had at my telling of our escape from Poland.

That I had received a failing grade again was an old story, but that my classmates had such interest in something I had fabricated was something new. It easily neutralized the grade failure and left me with a definite feeling of satisfaction.

After that, I discovered that whenever I read a story or an essay of mine in class, the effect on my classmates was markedly different than it was when other people read. And I realized that my suspicion about my stories being superior to those of my classmates was grounded in truth. My spelling, of course, continued to hang around my neck like a dead albatross, but I found that not only were my stories better, but that I could see ways that other people's stories could be improved as well. If Penfield had written, "They tossed her in the back of the rusty old truck," instead of, "She was put in a truck," his story would have had more punch. Or if in Schroder's story someone was in the bushes listening to Tom Straightshooter lay out his plan for capturing the bandits the next time they tried to rob a bank, there would be a lot more suspense.

But when I approached Penfield or Schroder or anyone else at recess or over lunch and tried to share my suggestions, I invariably found them totally disinterested. Had I given them the advice earlier and helped them to a higher grade, that would have been different. But once the story had been turned in and graded my advice was neither useful nor appreciated. I didn't understand this. What could be more important than learning how to write a good story like Mark Twain or Jack London?

Well, maybe this was another way in which I was different from other people. Maybe writing stories was something in which I had a special interest and even a special ability. The way that Frank Norwood could throw a baseball over the plate almost every time, I had a special talent for putting word combinations onto paper. And possibly within my slow-reading, poor-spelling, derelict soul, there was the spark of a writer, and I had a capacity that someday might be recognized.

This meant that maybe I did have a future, after all. That someday I would be able to earn a living at writing. Engineering, medicine, law, banking, scientific research, all the careers to which my classmates looked forward, might well be unavailable to me, but telling stories or explaining ideas were things that I just might be able to do. That, when I grew up, maybe I would be able to take care of my mother, and Mother would see things that I had written appear in print and she would not have to work anymore and could finally be proud of me.

Sunday mornings the school rose at eight instead of seven, and we dressed in our blue suits, white shirts, and black shoes. Then there would be pancakes for breakfast, followed by Mrs. Smith wiping the syrup stains off your tie before a worship service at the Protestant church that happened to adjoin the school campus.

But not for me. While my schoolmates were putting on their blue suits and looking forward to pancakes and syrup, I and the two or three other Catholic boys were standing on the front steps, already in our blue suits, waiting to be picked up by Father Sullivan and his assistant, Tommy, and driven to church.

Father Sullivan said mass in three churches every Sunday, for which I gave him considerable credit. Ours was the first. It was tiny, holding maybe eighty thin people at the most. While Father Sullivan prepared himself for the service and heard confessions, Tommy would direct us in refilling votive candle holders, filling the water and wine cruets, and, in warm weather, swatting the wasps that flew in through the open windows and landed on the back of the pews. If an altar boy didn't show up, Tommy would don a lacy white surplice and assist Father at the altar.

During our travel to America, I had experienced two definite crises pertaining to spiritual identity. Kiki's Catholic teachings and my inherent Judaism had collided in conflict over possession of my soul and, in the process, pretty well wiped out each other's credibility. It was all, I had decided, a bunch of inconvenient mumbo jumbo. It was only Mother's continued pretense that sent me on this meaningless excursion every Sunday morning. And the longer I seemed to have to wait for my Sunday breakfast, the more meaningless the excursion became.

Kneeling there in church I knew I was being a fraud, but if there was a God, He would know that I was only doing this per His fifth commandment and honoring my mother. And, if there wasn't a God, well then who was to know? I certainly wasn't going to ever tell anyone.

Suffering my way through a ritual that held no meaning for me was old stuff. I had sat, stood, and knelt through mass in Poland, Hungary, Rome, and Barcelona. But now there was a new problem. Every few weeks, the other Catholic Rumsey boys confessed their sins before mass, and then marched up to the rail to take Holy Communion with the grownups . . . while I knelt in my pew maintaining a pious expression on my face.

One such Sunday, Father Sullivan asked me why I did not partake of this sacrament. I had an answer ready: because of the war, I had been unable to have my First Communion. Father sympathized with this and suggested that the problem could easily be corrected. For this, I had not prepared and had to think fast. "My mother's brother is a priest, Father," I explained. "We come from a long line of priests, and it is a family tradition that we receive First Communion from an uncle or a grandfather. My mother won't let me take my First Communion from anyone but my uncle, and he is still in Europe . . . somewhere." That I had placed the blame for this problem on my mother's Catholic shoulders I considered a stroke of genius. For his part, Father Sullivan said something about my immortal soul with an unhappy look on his face, but he dropped the matter.

When we returned to school, the other boys would be attending their church service while we were served pancakes downstairs in the kitchen staff's dining room. The pancakes were quite stiff by this time, and, with no masters to supervise, you could easily roll one the length of the table and we found endless enjoyment in doing so. Then, after breakfast, one of the older Catholic boys, Richard, and I would engage in a foot race.

That a fifth former would seek me out from the other four or five boys was flattering, but the fact that he wanted me to go to his room and get into bed with him sounded weird. I had no idea what that was about, and I preferred to not find out. Consequently, as soon as our meal was over, I would dash across the empty side lawn toward the door of the Protestant church, sometimes with Richard in clumsy pursuit. While he was bigger than I was, Richard was also quite fat. Once inside the church, I could slip into one of the rear pews and join in the hymn singing, knowing that I was safe for another week.

My third summer in America, the Szyks rented a house in the town of Westport, Connecticut. Westport was on the coast, and the house was on the shore of Old Mill Pond, a little inlet of Long Island Sound.

The summer house reminded me of the cottage Mother and I had stayed at in southern Poland after our midnight escape from Warsaw. It had been a guest cottage on a farm belonging to some acquaintances, and it was where we stayed during the first weeks of the war.

The farm was worked by peasants living in similar thatch-roofed cottages. There was no electricity and water came from a hand pump at the kitchen sink. The toilet was in a little shack some meters behind each cottage. For a bed, my cousin Fredek, who was six months younger than I and whom I disliked, shared with me a dough-rolling stand in the kitchen/dining/living room.

Fredek and I had been given a job, the first of our lives: tending to the bulky wooden icebox in the kitchen. Twice a day a large, flat tray of melted ice had to be carefully removed from under the icebox and emptied into the wooden sink. And every second day, a cake of ice had to be fetched from the icehouse in a wheelbarrow.

We quickly learned that four eager hands carrying a large flat tray full of water or pushing a single wheelbarrow loaded with a slippery cake of ice, were two hands too many. We negotiated a more workable arrangement between the two of us. In addition to now having responsibilites, we now had more freedoms. We could walk about the farm without adult supervision or even asking for permission to do so. And, one day, we had even discovered the ecstasy of leaping from barn rafters into piles of hay. In my mind, until that summer of 1943 in Westport, those few weeks had been tied for the happiest of my life with the months of day school in New York.

As I looked at the wood plank doors and simple latches of the Westport bungalow, the little bedrooms, and the unpretentious furniture, I was reminded of that farm cottage of three years earlier. The fact that this one had electricity, running water, and an indoor toilet did not detract from the essential charm. While there were no horses, barn, or icebox, there was the pond that, at high tide, came almost to the front porch. And in place of the irritating Fredek there were the three Marrs.

Jules, Ann, and Charlie Marr were nephews and niece of a Polish man named Joe whom my cousin Alice had recently married. They had come from Krakow, Poland's medieval capital. Jules was a year older than me, Ann a year younger, and Charlie a year or two younger than Ann.

Besides being a year older than I, Jules had a more acceptable version of my own first name. My two years at Rumsey had not mitigated the image I held of "Julian" as a pudgy boy with a large nose looking back at me from the mirror. While hardly a monosyllabic "Jim" or "Mike" or "Sam," "Jules" would have made a perfectly acceptable compromise. (Eventually Jules Marr would become J. William "Bill" Marr.)

Unlike the boys at Rumsey, Jules did not hold my inferior age against me. While he was stronger and could pin me when we wrestled on the double bed that we were given to share, I could run and swim faster than he. Ann seemed to defer quite naturally to my greater age and wisdom, and little Charlie, small even for his age, seemed happy to be the group clown. There was less ego and more genuine friendship in our group of four than I had ever encountered. Combined with the water at our doorstep, clams for the digging, ice cream and fishing lines at the general store across the street, and Mother a good hour's train ride away in New York—where she could not tell me to comb my hair or flush toilets more quietly—this turned into the new best period of my life.

The one regrettable moment was when Jules's parents came for a weekend and Mr. Marr came into Jules's and my room to hear his son's evening prayer. As apparently was his custom, Jules placed a pillow over his head and began reciting in Hebrew, and I burst out laughing. Mr. Marr informed me that this was serious business, and I was utterly mortified.

Chapter Six

During Christmas vacation of that year, I met Mother's new friend, Pierre. Pierre was French, wore the uniform of a French Marines captain, and walked on one leg and a pair of aluminum crutches. He had lost his left leg in Africa, fighting alongside General de Gaulle against the German general Erwin Rommel, whose name we all well knew. General de Gaulle, Mother explained to me, since Pierre spoke little English and my French vocabulary was limited to more mundane matters, was leader of the Free French, those Frenchmen who had not gone over to the side of the Germans earlier in the war. Pierre had been one of the few men who had followed the general into the Allied ranks. Pierre was, she said, a highly decorated hero who had been sent to America to make speeches promoting the sale of war bonds and to have an artificial leg fitted. Pierre had a round face, black hair parted in the middle, and a moustache. He was handsome and friendly.

One of the things I had recently learned at Rumsey was that whenever I saw a man and a woman of Mother's approximate age together, I should assume that they were "doing it." What doing it actually constituted I had no idea, except that it was something that no one was to know about. Divining it in the case of Mother and Pierre made me pretty *hep*. It was also, I was sure, something that was in some kind of conflict with whatever it was that went on between Mother and Reggie. Since Pierre was much more likable than the old man, I resolved never to tell the latter.

The first time I met Pierre was when he came to visit Mother on the second day of my vacation and took us out to dinner. At dinner, Mother announced that she couldn't spend time with either of us the following afternoon since she had business to attend to, and was there any chance that Pierre could take me to the movies? I loved going to the movies, but I couldn't imagine this Frenchman, with his limited English, agreeing to such an afternoon. I had been to some French movies with my mother and understood little despite a certain fluency in the language that I had acquired in our travels, and I rated Pierre's English considerably below my French. To my very great surprise, Pierre said that he loved American movies and that he considered them a big help in learning the language. Was there a movie I could recommend for the two of us to see?

Here I had a problem. As a grownup, he would most likely want to see some romance, while what I really wanted to see was the new Abbott and Costello film. I had dragged Mother to the previous Abbott and Costello production, one in which the two are in flight school, and Mother had pronounced it plain silly and a total waste of both our time. I could not imagine Pierre enjoying this one any more than she did. On the other hand, I didn't know any romances to recommend, did I? So, really, the only choice I had for tomorrow was Abbott and Costello.

On the way home from the restaurant, Mother stopped the taxi on Broadway, two blocks from our apartment, where a man was selling Christmas trees on the corner. She and I got out to select a tree, and Mother instructed Pierre to stay in the taxi with his crutches. It had rained and the pavement was slippery. As Mother and I picked a tree and then negotiated for it, I could see Pierre's discomfort at not being able to be of assistance. He was sitting at the open taxi door, his two crutches in one hand outside the taxi, hoping to be called to assist. It was the first time I could remember seeing a grownup I knew in such a helpless situation, and I felt sorry for him.

The cabby put the tree in the trunk, and we drove on. Up in our apartment, Pierre asked for some wood, nails, and a hammer to build a stand for the tree. I was sorry to disappoint him by producing our old fold-up metal stand from the top shelf in the coat closet. Then, Pierre lay on the floor to screw the stand tight to the tree as I held it upright and Mother gave me left and right directions.

The next afternoon, Pierre picked me up at our apartment and we took a taxi to the theater. I heard him struggling with his English as he purchased an adult ticket and a children's for the loge, where he would be permitted to smoke. Unlike today, when we check for a start time, in those days movies ran continually. The custom was to walk in at any time and stay until that same scene was reached the next time around. Then you would whisper, "This is where we came in," to your companion and slip out quietly.

The film was a disappointment to me—I considered the humor forced as compared to the previous Abbott and Costello film. I, of course, wasn't familiar with the term *forced* as applied to humor, but I was quite certain in my judgment and proud of my maturity. Pierre, on the other hand, enjoyed it tremendously, laughing with all the other kids in the theater. The second feature was some kind of commando film, which we seemed to enjoy equally. Then we had dinner in a restaurant again and, finally, we returned to the apartment, where we waited for Mother to return and join us.

As we sat in the living room looking at each other, I desperately wanted to think of something to talk about. I ruled out such gambits as, "Wasn't that a good movie?" or, "Did you see the previous Abbott and Costello film?" as too obvious and not leading to much in the way of a response. I could see that Pierre felt as awkward about this as I did. He smoked his Chesterfield cigarettes and smiled whenever our eyes met.

I thought I saw Pierre wince; I wasn't sure. But a minute later he winced again, and I realized something had hurt him. "Ze feengers from my foote, zey 'urt me," he explained, pointing to his nonexistent left foot. I nodded without comprehending. "May I 'ave some Scotch, please?" he asked.

Mother had a brass-and-glass cart, on the bottom shelf of which she kept a quantity of liquor bottles though she, herself, had little tolerance for alcohol and drank only in company and never more than one glass. There was a bottle with the picture of a white horse and the word *Scotch* on the label. I held it up and Pierre nodded from his chair. I took out a glass and began pouring into it.

"Stop!" I heard Pierre call, when I had poured maybe half an inch. I stopped and saw him holding his hand up. "Ice and ze soda, please," Pierre said, putting the accent on the second syllable of *soda*. I could tell that he was biting back another pang of pain.

The Scotch, I realized, must have some analgesic value and hurried through the apartment to the kitchen for ice cubes. There were a number of bottles of club soda on the bottom shelf of the bar, and I quickly opened one and poured some into the glass.

"*Encore*," Pierre said, which I knew meant *more* in French. He accompanied it with a thumbs down motion of his right hand into his left fist. He was miming soda being poured liberally.

I poured more soda till I saw him raise his thumb. The glass was so full I was afraid of spilling it and was as pale as plain soda water. Pierre was already holding his hand out as I carried it carefully across the floor. He took a sip immediately and sighed. He nodded in gratitude then settled back in his chair. "Sank you," he said.

Judging by the anxiety with which he had awaited his Scotch, I expected Pierre to be requesting a refill soon. He had had a Scotch and soda with dinner, and I knew that some men drank large quantities of the stuff. But I was surprised to see that, following his initial sip, Pierre only took tiny sips every few minutes. The Scotch seemed to be easing his pain in the nonexistant foot. And I was having, I realized, a very educational experience.

When Mother burst through the front door—Mother always entered in that fashion unless she was "deathly tired"—Pierre's glass was still half full and I was leafing through a copy of *Vogue*, a very unsatisfying exercise.

The next day was Christmas Eve, and when I learned that Pierre would be coming over again I asked whether we would be opening presents that evening while Pierre was there or the next morning. Mother said that we would open them that evening, and my next question was whether we had one for Pierre. Mother assured me that she did.

Of course, without an allowance I didn't have the ability to buy a present for anyone, so I had to ask Mother for money to buy her one. She gave me five dollars and directed me to Woolworth's, a few blocks away, where she said I should buy her a dust mop. Had I had a Christmas gift list for Mother, a dust mop would not have been on it, but, since that was what Mother wanted, that was what she would get. I put on my jacket and set out for Woolworth's.

I had sixteen cents left over after I'd made my purchase. With the money I could have bought a comic book *and* a Milky Way bar, but then the idea of a gift for Pierre presented itself. Mother had said that she had bought him a present, but I doubted that there was anyone else in New York with one for him. I bought a pack of Chesterfield cigarettes from a sidewalk magazine stand and pocketed the final four cents. I skipped all the way home.

Mother was taking a bath when I got home, so I put the mop and the cigarettes under the tree and looked for something to do in the little apartment. When Mother came out of the bathroom, she gave me five dollars more and sent me to the delicatessen a few blocks away for three smoked salmon and cream cheese sandwiches. Pierre, she said, was coming for lunch. When I came back Mother was still in her bathrobe, smoking a cigarette on the living room sofa. The pack I had laid under the tree for Pierre was gone.

I was heartbroken. I knew I could have explained the situation to Mother and asked for another twelve cents, but I could well imagine how humiliated she would feel at her mistake. I debated the issue for some time, weighing Pierre's loneliness in a strange country against Mother's embarrassment. Pierre's loneliness won out in the end, because it would last considerably longer.

"Mother," I said, addressing her in English. We normally spoke Polish to one another, but since my English was considerably better than hers I felt myself on more equal footing in that language. "I know that there was no way for you to know this, but the cigarettes that were there under the tree were for Pierre for Christmas."

"Oh, I'm sorry," Mother said, laughing. "Why don't you go and get him another pack. Bring me my purse."

I was so incredibly glad that Mother had such a good sense of humor. I laughed in relief. That evening I received a metal helmet, just like the ones American soldiers wore, from Mother, and a model airplane kit, a P-40, from Pierre. But I was most happy about the cigarettes I could give Pierre and about the laugh I had shared with Mother, earlier.

It seemed that Pierre came to visit Mother every afternoon of my two-week vacation. He didn't know anyone else in New York, she explained. And on two more such afternoons, he and I went to the movies while Mother attended to business. Both times I was the one to select the movie. I picked two westerns, which Pierre seemed to enjoy as much as I did.

Pierre also helped me to build my P-40. I didn't really want his help—I had built similar airplanes before—but Pierre insisted that his help was needed, and Mother directed me to watch and to learn from him. Soon I was looking over Pierre's shoulder and cringing as he cut bulkheads out of balsa with my Exacto knife and cemented things together, often splitting the fragile wood or cementing it in the wrong place or in the wrong position. He tended to misunderstand the instructions and swore a lot in French. I was sure that Mother's other friend, Reggie, would have allowed me to build my own airplane.

What made me forgive Pierre for taking over my model airplane was his love of France. I didn't love France—I loved America—but the way Pierre spoke about what he would do in his home country once the war was over made me admire him a lot. Before the war, he said, there had been great selfishness and corruption in the French government, and this had led to France's "error." When the war was over, General de Gaulle would change all that and Pierre would be there to help him.

Mother explained to me how much General de Gaulle liked Pierre and how highly the French people respected their wounded soldiers, which would give Pierre a powerful weapon once he ran for a government office. I understood that. In addition to all that, she said, Pierre was a wonderful public speaker, speaking with a passion that attracted and convinced people, even when he spoke his Pidgin English, and I could well see him as a French Franklin Roosevelt in the making.

I didn't see Pierre during spring vacation because Reggie was back in town. He and Mother went out to dinner and lunch a lot, but without me. One evening as Reggie sat on our sofa waiting for Mother to dress, his bulk spilling over the arm rest, I was reading a comic book on the floor. I saw him gesture to me to come over, and I got up and crossed the room. I saw Reggie peel some money off a roll that wouldn't have fit in a smaller man's pocket and hand it to me. It was a hundred dollar bill. He didn't say a word during the transaction, not even to be careful how I spent it or to give it to Mother to put in the bank for me.

With that hundred dollar bill I bought a used electric train—they weren't making any new ones "for the duration"—and a used bicycle. Each came to around fifty dollars. There were new bicycles available for about half that price, but you had to have a doctor's prescription to buy one.

Chapter Seven

The following summer, Mother and I were on a train to Reno, Nevada, which was where people all went to get divorced in those days. Nevada, apparently, had very liberal divorce laws. Once you had established a six-week uninterrupted residency, you were entitled to partake of this liberality.

We had learned recently that Mother's husband, my stepfather Lolek, was being held in a German prisoner of war camp. While I had never had much liking for Lolek, I knew that the lot of prisoners of war was not a pleasant one and sending him a letter through the Red Cross telling him that she had just divorced him did not seem like a patriotic thing for Mother to be doing. The need to be supportive of our troops was much in the news these days, and I didn't think Mother's divorce was in that spirit.

When Mother informed me that most people did their six-week residency at what was called a *dude ranch* and we would be spending our stay on horseback, my concern for Lolek's feelings diminished somewhat. I could not believe that my old dream of horses, cowboys, and lariats was finally about to come true. My tolerance of Mother improved a bit.

Our trip was all being financed, of course, by Reggie, and the first night was on the famous Twentieth Century

Limited, speeding between Grand Central and Chicago. Just as it is depicted in films, we walked along a red carpet down the platform to our sleeping car. Our compartment had an upper and a lower berth, and dinner in the dining car was served by smiling "colored" waiters in long white aprons. We spent one day in Chicago, and the next day we were on another train bound for the West Coast.

This second train, however, was quite different from the previous one. This being wartime, soldiers, sailors, and munitions were being shipped westward for combat in the Pacific, so train reservations were difficult to come by. Travel was on a need-to-go basis. The best that Mr. Purbrick's money and influence had been able to procure was two seats that converted into an upper and a lower for the night. Young men in uniform and a few civilians, traveling on defense business, filled every seat. The sound of guitars, ukuleles, harmonicas, and male voices in song filled each car for most waking hours.

And it was hot. This was July, and the train wasn't air-conditioned. There were many stops along the way, some scheduled but most not. We were not, as our conductor explained, a "priority train" and frequently had to yield our track to one with tanks or artillery pieces fastened to flatcars, which I saw speeding past my window. Some of our stops were several hours long, and I could see soldiers and sailors from our train playing catch with a baseball in the field beside the train. I had a baseball glove in my suitcase and wanted to go out and join them, but Mother wouldn't let me. She did let me open the window, though.

I saw one sailor who, the others were saying, was a pitcher with a Red Sox farm team, throwing to a soldier with a catcher's mitt. The sailor had taken off his jacket and the soldier his shirt, and I could see the sweat stains growing on their undershirts. A small crowd had gathered around to watch as the sailor went through elaborate windups, kicked his leg high in the air, and hurled the ball with a perfectly flat trajectory. I could hear it pop into the glove. It was the first time I had seen a professional baseball player, and afterward I looked for him on the train, but he must have been in some other car.

Sometimes we reversed direction and headed back toward Chicago to get onto a side track and let a priority train whip by. How long the entire trip would take was anybody's guess.

Mother was the only woman in our car, and there were usually several soldiers or sailors in and around our little space, admiring Mother's long legs as she, a copy of her book in her hands, told and retold the story of our escape or answered questions about Poland and Paris and Berlin. The GIs were all extremely courteous, treating Mother as a celebrity and addressing her, mostly, as Mrs. Padarewski.

At the beginning of our third night on the train, I was sitting cross-legged at the foot of Mother's lower bunk, watching her lay out a solitaire, a cigarette in her mouth, when we heard singing on the other side of the curtain. Apparently several GIs who had had a little too much to drink were making their way down the aisle, trying to harmonize in a song called "Sweet Genevieve." I saw Mother smile at their efforts.

Then there was the angry voice of a conductor telling them that they couldn't do this, that they would wake the other passengers, and that he would call the military police at the next station.

Suddenly, I saw Mother climbing out of the bunk. I, of course, followed and saw her, in her sheer nightie and bare feet, a furious expression on her face, telling the conductor that these soldiers were on their way to board ships to fight the Japanese in the Pacific, and if they wanted to pass their travel time singing, he was "hell as sure" going to let them do it. There were heads and then bare feet popping out of the curtains all down the aisle, and the conductor backed off from his threats. And soon a pajama-and-underwear-clad chorus was singing of *Genevieve, sweet Genevieve,* eventually changing to *Oh, Barbara, sweet Barbara.*

I did not see the conductor make his exit but in a few moments all the curtains had been drawn back, from one end of the car to the other, and Mother, with her tone-deaf voice, was leading a rendition of "Frere Jacques." I watched a young man, in his olive-drab, government issue undershirt and shorts, wipe the top of a whiskey bottle vigorously with a handkerchief, then hand it to Mother. For the only time in my life, I saw Mother lift the bottle to her lips. I suspect, though, that she did not actually drink. Mother tolerated alcohol very poorly, and would grow violently ill after a few glasses of wine.

A wooden-sided station wagon with WHISPERING PINES lettered on the side, picked us and another woman up at the Reno train station to take us to the dude ranch. The other woman, black hair held on top of her head with bobby pins, introduced herself to Mother as Mrs. Stenger and offered her a cigarette. Mother accepted, and they discussed the things that women bent on divorce talk about while they smoke cigarettes. I looked out the window at men and women in ten-gallon hats, jeans, and high-heeled boots walking in the Reno streets. Then, outside of town, we passed a group of similarly dressed men and women on horseback riding single file alongside the highway. I watched for Indians, bison, or wild horses but didn't see any.

The ranch, which I expected to be adobe huts surrounded by cactus, turned out to be a series of log cabins in a forest of pines. There was, however, a corral, empty at the moment, and several horses and a donkey grazing in a field across the road.

A woman about Mother's age introduced herself as Dorothy, welcomed us to Whispering Pines, and informed us that "we are all on a first name basis here." Mrs. Stenger seemed to have some difficulty revealing her name to be Louise. Older than Mother and Dorothy, she did not appear comfortable with the first-name arrangement.

Mother and I were assigned a cabin with two bedrooms, a living room, and a bath. Meals, we were told, were served family style in the main cabin, and we were just in time for lunch. We were issued cloth napkins and clothespins. We were to write our first names on the clothespins to identify our napkins for future use. As I had suspected she would, after the meal I found that Louise had lettered "Mrs. Stenger" on hers. The grownups, most dressed in jeans and checked shirts, all ate at one long table while I, a boy my age named Paul, and a slightly younger girl named Fannie had a table to ourselves. Paul and Fannie had been horseback riding that morning and smelled of it a little.

After lunch, Dorothy drove Mother and me—Mrs. Stenger having declined—back into Reno to be outfitted with cowboy gear. I got jeans, a couple of checkered shirts, boots, and a ten-gallon hat. Mother did the same. I could not wait for the following morning to go horseback riding with Paul, Fannie, and Mother.

Dorothy had explained that Mother and I should report to the corral an hour before the scheduled ride to meet Pat, the wrangler, and be checked out on our riding skills. I had ridden on a few pony rides, both in New York's Central Park and back in Warsaw, but I had never been on a full-sized horse that wasn't being led by an attendant and

I was nervous. Mother had a headache the next morning and told me that I should go to the corral by myself.

Pat was a small, thin man with weathered skin and a smile. He introduced me to a white horse named Alice. Alice, he informed me, was twenty years old and very gentle. But she was quite tall, and, much to my embarrassment, I had to stand on a box in order to get my left foot into the stirrup.

Alice responded to the commands that Pat showed me to use with my left hand (the right hand, I knew, had to be free to throw the lariat or shoot a gun) and the heels of my boots. After a few walks and trots around the corral, I was pronounced qualified to join the other *dudes* in that morning's ride.

Our rides were along trails up and down mountains, which I found a little scary. There were spots where I would have much preferred to get down and lead Alice on foot and even on all fours up the shaley rocks. A woman named Beverly saw me holding onto the saddle horn and told me I shouldn't do that. She showed me how to adjust my behind in the saddle and my legs in the stirrups for balance. "Watch my behind," she told me. Beverly was the same age as Mother, and watching her behind as it moved to the horse's rhythm was a treat. Soon I had forgotten to be afraid.

Pat always rode one of his own horses. He owned two of them, one named Chico, the other Amigo. Chico was a palomino, gold colored with blond tail and mane, and Amigo was a dappled gray. In place of a regular bridle, Pat's horses wore a bridle made of woven horsehair without a bit. He told me it was called a *hackamore*, and he used it because both his horses were very young and he didn't want them to get a "hard mouth" from the bit. I could see how carefully and gently he rode his horses, how subtle his motions were and how willingly the horses responded to his touch. I had never seen anything or anyone treated so gently before.

In a few days I was promoted to a horse named Rocket. He was brown and a little smaller than Alice, but I could tell he had more life to him. I could feel his eagerness to run, but except for the half mile or so between the ranch and where our trails began, the way was too steep or too narrow to do anything but walk. On the way to the trail we would sometimes trot, an unpleasant, bone-jolting gait. I had seen riders back East and in Europe posting up and down in the saddle to dampen the jarring, but I knew from books that one did not post in a Western saddle.

Then one day as we left the trail for the straight stretch back to the ranch, I heard Pat shout, "Don't . . . don't let him run!" to me. But the warning had come just a beat too late because Rocket was lighting out for home with considerable interest.

I pulled back on the reins, but that didn't seem to dampen his enthusiasm to any recognizable degree. Suddenly I found myself as though in a rocking chair as my horse stretched out his legs in a canter and then a gallop for home. We flew beside the road, turned the corner into the ranch driveway, and scattered gravel with a satisfying crunch.

Until Rocket arrived at the closed gate to the corral and stopped. I did not.

I did not sail over the gate, as Lou Costello would certainly have done. I landed, instead, in the tall grass at the foot of the corral on my hands, knees, and shoulder. In a moment, people from the main building were running out to tend to me, but the only tending necessary was to my ego. I dearly hoped that Beverly had been too far behind me to see my five-point, tail-high landing.

As I assured everyone that I was all right, I saw Pat standing beside me, holding my horse. "Get back on," he commanded.

There were immediate protests from the women who had rushed to my rescue.

"No, he's hurt."

"He's frightened."

"That's cruel."

"Let the boy rest a little."

"Do it tomorrow."

Pat didn't say anything, but kept looking at me. I understood that this was a matter between us men. I wasn't afraid to get back onto Rocket's back. It wasn't as though he had bucked me off deliberately. He had just stopped when I hadn't prepared for it. Next time such a thing happened, I would realize that he had to stop at the closed gate and be ready. Next time, I wouldn't let him run on the way back to the corral. I took the reins from Pat's hand, stuck my foot in the stirrup, and hoisted myself back up.

Suddenly I heard clapping. The people from the main building and the ones I had been riding with were applauding what I had done. I had never been applauded before.

Mother had not come riding the second day, as she had promised, nor the third day nor the fourth. She did put on her jeans after Dorothy showed her how form-fitting they became after a washing. It was after three or four weeks of urging from me that she finally put on the boots and the hat and walked down to the corral with me after breakfast.

"He is so big," she said in Polish as Pat led Alice to the mounting block on which Mother was standing.

"She's very gentle," I assured her, deliberately responding in English. "She's the first horse I rode too." I held the stirrup for her. "Here, hold here when you mount, but then don't hold it again," I said, indicating the saddle horn.

"I will come back tomorrow," Mother said.

I gave Pat a look that I hoped indicated my total disengagement from this development. He said nothing.

"You're here now, Barbara," a voice from behind me said, and I realized that several of the women were standing at the rail watching.

"Go ahead," someone else said.

Mother looked around at them and gave a shy smile. I didn't think that I had ever seen a genuinely shy look on Mother's face before. She put both hands on the saddle horn and placed her left foot in the stirrup. With an ease I hadn't expected to see, she swung her right leg over the horse's rump and settled into the saddle. Pat handed her the reins and gave instructions regarding go, stop, turn left, and turn right. Then he stepped away from Alice and instructed Mother to move her forward.

I saw Mother's heels press Alice's sides lightly. But Alice did not move. I was sure that the same nudge from me had produced positive results. Pat clucked his tongue. "Come on, Alice," he said. Alice moved slowly forward.

I saw Mother move her hand shakily to the right, to direct Alice toward the center of the corral. But the move was almost imperceptible to me, and I wondered how much had gotten through to the horse. Alice continued walking in a straight line.

"Pull a little harder, Barbara," Pat said.

Mother's hand jerked slightly.

"Don't jerk," Pat said. "Just lay your hand over toward your knee."

Mother gave several more little jerks. Alice did not respond.

"She doesn't want to," Mother said.

"Tell her she has to," Pat said.

Mother's hand jerked slightly again.

"She doesn't want to," Mother repeated.

"All right, Barbara, stop her," Pat said.

Mother looked at him, uncomprehending, and I could see the tension in her face.

"Whoa, Alice," Pat said, and the white horse stopped.

"Let me have that stirrup," Pat said, indicating Mother's left stirrup. Mother looked down in confusion.

The wrangler gently pulled Mother's boot out of the stirrup. He put his own foot in the empty stirrup, grabbed the horn and swung himself into position behind the saddle. He put his hand over Mother's and clucked Alice into motion. "Like this," he said, moving the reins to the left.

Alice turned immediately.

"And like this," he said, turning her to the right. "Now you try it."

"I . . . I don't want to," Mother pleaded. "I want to get down."

Pat stopped Alice and helped Mother down.

"I . . . I will try a different day. Thank you very much." Mother never mounted a horse again.

Chapter Eight

In my fifth form year, the fourth year I was at Rumsey, my roommate was a fourth former named Tony. Rooming with an "inferior" was a somewhat different experience for me than sharing housekeeping with a peer. Whereas with Bob Carroll or Rod Hodgins many of my ideas and suggestions regarding such things as rearranging our room furniture had been up for discussion, whatever I suggested to Tony was usually enacted, if only until it proved impractical.

Thus it was that I undertook, as I would never have dared with my previous roommates, to tell Tony stories about my prewar life in Poland. But it wasn't life as I had lived it. It was life based mostly on several movies we had seen. I told him about living in a castle, complete with ghost, dressing in a tuxedo every night for dinner, owning my own horse and race car as well as a tame bear named Mischief. Each night, after lights out, I would turn toward Tony and, whispering across the room, begin spinning a totally spontaneous tale of adventures with Mischief or my race car or my horse.

That Tony should believe these outrageous lies did not cease to amaze me. Particularly in view of the reception my true story had received at the hands of Mr. Gregg. What I did not wonder at in the slightest was my own ability to spontaneously produce these yarns night after night. And it wasn't until I had begun my post-retirement writing career some sixty years later that I recalled this snippet of my young life with something like amazement. As for Tony's gullibility, I now realize that his attitude must have been more one of, *If this idiot insists on keeping me entertained with his fantasies, why should I stop him?*

Then it was a May morning of the following calendar year, 1945, and Madame Allagrant, teacher of French, came running into the school building, where I had a study hall period. "Ze Germans . . . 'ave . . . surrendered," she said, between breaths from the back of the room. "Ze war in Europe, . . . she is *fini!*"

There was cheering from the boys in study hall, and soon heads began to appear from upstairs. "The war in Europe is over!" we explained and soon more cheering could be heard throughout the building as boys and masters came running down the stairs.

I spent that summer back in Westport. The Szyks had bought a house now. Their daughter Alice, her husband Joe, and their daughters Katherine and Jeanie lived there the year round, while Uncle Arthur and Aunt Julia came out on weekends. Jules's sister Ann was there that summer as well, and I don't remember where Jules and Charlie were, though not with us in Westport.

This house was a distance from the water but sat on what I would estimate at half an acre of land. In back, there was Alice's victory garden, and Alice directed Ann and me to spend our mornings weeding this garden and performing other agricultural activities. While I understood the need to mow the grass, it was also my belief that with our troops already victorious in Europe and the Japanese surrendering island after island in the Pacific, a victory garden was superfluous and should be operated on a strictly volunteer basis.

Cousin Alice disagreed. When I asked what parts of my logic she disagreed with, she refused to engage me and simply informed me that her original directions were to be taken as orders. As Ann and I knelt amid the young vegetables, pulling grass and weeds out of the ground, I went to great lengths explaining to my fellow indentured laborer how my Cousin Alice, Ann's aunt by marriage, was neither a compassionate nor an intelligent person. What I didn't know was that Alice mustn't have been much of a gardener either, since I don't recall any produce from that garden ever making its way to our table.

Ann was an amiable summer companion. I was thirteen and she, probably twelve. We slept on the second floor, where Ann had a room and I had a couch in the large loft area at the top of the stairs. There was another bedroom for weekend guests and a bathroom. One of the weekend guests that summer was an attractive blonde woman named Stella Adler, an actress, close friend of the Szyks, and recognized by many as the finest acting teacher in Hollywood.

A railing surrounded the stairwell on three sides, and Ann and I would spend an hour or so each night in our pajamas, after being directed to bed, leaning on this railing and talking quietly across the stairwell. What we talked about I do not remember, except that she found my highly embellished accounts of life at Rumsey very interesting.

Jules's little sister did not arouse my anatomical interests the way grown women did. She was simply a pleasant summer companion whom I taught to ride a two-wheeler in the road in front of the house. I also taught her to throw and catch a baseball though, try as she might, she could not follow my directions and throw the ball properly. I remember getting angry at her klutziness.

That I could get angry at Ann without fear of retribution was an experience that was both pleasurable and disquieting. That it released considerable accumulated frustration was something of which I was aware. But I was also well aware of the humiliation that my younger housemate must be suffering under my tutelage. One day, as she rode on the crossbar of my bicycle on our way to the movies in town, the heel of Ann's sandal got caught in the spokes of my front wheel, sending us both over the handlebars and aborting our movie trip. Despite her profuse apologies, I bawled her out as I had seen Mr. Sherry, the Rumsey director/football coach bawling out receivers who dropped passes. I didn't speak to her for several days after that.

Then it was December 1945, and I carried my suitcase along the train platform looking for Mother. I always looked forward to our greeting at the station. However distracted Mother might get as our time together wore on, her greetings in Grand Central were always warm and, I believed, pretty genuine.

Earlier, I might have been alarmed at not seeing her, but now I knew that if we did manage to miss each other or if she had been unavoidably detained, I could always heft my suitcase to our new apartment on East Sixty-Third Street on foot, even if I might have to stop to rest along the way. With no use for cash at Rumsey, I had no allowance and, therefore, no means of taking a Madison Avenue bus. But I was big enough now to cope with such things.

Then Mother's friend Lilly was standing there on the platform, smiling nervously. She greeted me and offered a powdered cheek to kiss. Lilly was a single woman, a friend of the family, and a former professional singer who had ruined her voice by performing against doctor's orders some time before the war. She was American but had been brought up in Poland and was faultlessly fluent in both languages. It was she who had taken me to see the story of Lou Gehrig, *Pride of the Yankees*, at Radio City Music Hall when I was just beginning to understand baseball.

"Mother's in England," Lilly now explained in English. There was, I now realized, a strong flavor of Manhattan in her speech. Of Mother's friends that I had met, either European or American, Lilly was the only one who spoke with a true New York accent. "I'm going to put you on a plane this evening so you can join her for Christmas," she concluded.

I, of course, had had no inkling of Mother's trip. Despite my pleas in the compulsory letters we wrote home every Sunday, Mother never responded. Where she might be at any given time or what she might be doing was nothing I expected ever to know. Some hours later, with Lilly's assurances that Mother would be waiting at the airport in London, I was strapped in, chewing a Chiclets distributed before takeoff by the attractive stewardess, and speeding down the runway for the first time in my life.

If I was afraid of this long voyage by myself, I did not permit myself to feel it. I had on a gray double-breasted suit that Mrs. Smith had gone over with a damp sponge for gravy spots before we boarded our train in Cornwall, and I considered myself as fully grown up as my fellow passengers. In fact, I was envious of the stewardesses in their blue uniforms with gold wings pinned to their front, who moved around the airplane tending to passengers while I had to sit strapped into my seat. An elderly woman (thirty, if she was a day) strapped in beside me smiled nervously at me, and I thrust my jaw forward, assuring her that we had things under control.

Within seconds I was looking down on the lights of New York, and within minutes I was ready to throw up my insides.

"Oh, the poor kiddy's ill," a kindly British-accented lady near me said, adding to my embarrassment. There was concern in her voice and on the part of several other passengers, many with similar British accents.

At first I took umbrage at this affront. I was not a *kiddy*, but a thirteen-year-old American, perfectly capable of traveling on his own. Then somebody said, "There's a paper bag in the pocket in front of you," and I reached for it gratefully, filling it immediately.

Instantly, a stewardess was there to replace it with a fresh one.

"He'll feel much better now," a voice said. The kindly woman was lying through her teeth. I did not feel better till we had wheels on the ground at Gander Air Force Base in Newfoundland for refueling hours later.

It was deep into the night at this point, and it was snowing. We would not be able to take off again, we were told, until the snow stopped. We would be transported to the base Officers' Club where we could entertain ourselves until the weather had cleared.

What I wanted now wasn't entertainment but food. Dinner on the plane had been out of the question and anything I might have ingested since breakfast had been cleaned out of my stomach hours ago. I was hungry as only a teenager can be hungry. But I didn't have a cent in my pocket. My fellow passengers were ordering hamburgers, sandwiches, and drinks in the Officers' Club lounge, and I sat there with my insides gnawing at me, waving aside waiters with menus. It would occur to me, years later, that the airline was, most likely, picking up the tab at the Officers' Club. But nobody had told me.

The rest of the flight was only half as bad as the first part. Having eaten a hearty in-flight breakfast, I did not throw it up for a good hour. Then I sat, defiant in my misery, allowing the stewardess and the older woman seated beside me to tuck a blanket around me. I stayed that way all the way to Shannon in Ireland where we stopped for more fuel.

By the time we took off on our final leg to London, I was pretty well conditioned to air travel. Only we weren't going to London. Weather was again the villain, and we were headed for Christchurch in Scotland. We would take the train to London in the morning.

We had dinner on the airplane, and it did not seem to bother me. My hotel room in Christchurch was decent enough and my roommate, a bald man of middle age, never uttered a word.

We were wakened for breakfast and my order of scrambled eggs was met with regret. The hotel had no eggs—eggs were scarce in Britain. What it did, in fact, have was a choice between *herring* and *kippers*. Herring was a fish I had eaten with onions and sour cream and was not my idea of breakfast food. I opted for the mysterious kippers. Kippers, it turned out, were also a fish. I could not get a single bite down my throat.

Then we were on the train to London. When the conductor came by to collect tickets, I had none. It appeared that train tickets had been passed out at the hotel, but, again, no one had told me. Or, if they had, I hadn't heard. My compartment mates, all veterans of our flight, jumped to my defense. "The kiddy is coming home to England," they explained. "He was sent to America during the blitz and now he's come back. But somebody failed to give him his train ticket. See how American he speaks?"

"Aye, but it's home to London Town he's going now," somebody said.

The conductor took out his ticket-issuing paraphernalia and resolved the problem.

At the station in London Town, I looked for Mother on the platform, as I had at Grand Central two days earlier. Mother wasn't there either, but a uniformed hotel bellboy held a sign saying PADOWICY. I had learned long ago that any capitalized word approximating my name likely meant me. My mother, the bellboy explained, was waiting for me at the hotel. He took my bag and headed into the station. I hurried after him out into the street.

As we turned a corner, I had a shock. It was a sight that took me back to a night several years ago as my mother and I rode in the horse-drawn *doroszka* through blacked-out Warsaw streets to my Aunt Edna's house. A building had just had its front wall ripped off by a bomb, spilling its ruble across the street and exposing the multicolored rooms and hallways. Except that here in London, the building had been cleaned up and now stood there like an architectural feature. I suddenly remembered the bombing that England had undergone until just recently, but my heart was in my throat not over England's pain but the fact that it was on that very morning in Warsaw that I had discovered my nanny, Kiki, the only mother I had known to that time, suddenly gone from my life.

"Oh, I am so glad you're here, Julian" Mother said in Polish when my guide had delivered me to her suite. She fed me a scone and a cup of tea. "I need you to make an important decision."

I requested another scone.

"Reggie has said," Mother began, as she buttered me another scone, "that I either marry him now or forget it. And Pierre is here too, and says the same thing. I don't know what to do. Which one do you want to be your father?"

In truth, I did not consider either man to be father material. Reggie could have made a good grandfather. Not the kindly sort, but the aloof kind who gives good presents at Christmas. Pierre, on the other hand, was more of a little brother, pushing his way to my toys, needing sympathy for the painful "feengers from my foote" which weren't there, and language translation.

"Pierre wants to go back to France and go into politics," Mother continued, "but I'm not going to be a politician's wife. If I marry him, I will make him go into the diplomatic service. France owes him that for his leg."

I was beginning to feel sorry again for Pierre, but then my mother gave the clincher. "If I marry Reggie," she said, "I will have to stay here and you will fly back to America after Christmas. If I marry Pierre, the three of us will fly back together next Thursday."

Pierre's fate had just been sealed. "I like Pierre better," I said.

Mother and Pierre married a few days later at the French consulate. Reggie Purbrick gave the wedding reception for Georges Pierre and Barbara Gabard. I was invited to neither function, but stayed at the hotel playing gin rummy with an off-duty chambermaid. On the flight back to America I began to feel motion sickness the moment our pilot started the engines.

Chapter Nine

A younger boy interrupted our three-student Latin class. We were seniors now, but transfers and expulsions for smoking had pared our class down to just Bob Carroll, Rod Hodgins, and me. "There's a call for Padowicz in the office, sir," he said. "It's urgent."

I rushed from the school building to the main building, fearing for what I might hear. As I ran, I also speculated that, perhaps, the distance between these two buildings had never been crossed in so short a time. I was the fastest runner at Rumsey.

"Pierre and I are at the airport," Mother was saying in Polish. "We are flying to Lima in Peru. Pierre has been attached to the embassy there. Aunt Julia will come to your graduation dance. You'll go stay with them till I send for you. Obey everything she says."

I assured her that I would.

"Oh, and where do I have to send the check for your next school?"

Her question baffled me. The finances pertaining to my Rumsey schooling were all handled outside my realm of experience. That I should know the mailing address of my next school, when I hadn't even been told what school that would be, took me aback. "I don't even know where I'm going next year," I said.

"Shouldn't you know by now?" she asked.

Once more I was speechless. Yes, I should know by now—my two classmates had been told where they were going—but Mother hadn't deigned to notify me.

"Oh my God!" she protested at my silence. "You had better get going and take care of it. Tell Aunt Julia. She will notify me in Lima. Now I have to go, good-bye."

Standing there in the school office as the secretary cranked papers through a mimeograph copier, it gradually dawned on me that I had just been informed that choosing my next school would be up to me.

I knew the names of some secondary schools but knew nothing more about them. Bob, I knew, would be going to a school called Millbrook, where his older brother had gone. Our baseball team had played their midget team a few weeks earlier and I remembered some friendly looking brick buildings on a hill above the athletic field. We had even shaken hands with the headmaster, a tall man with a British accent who had reminded me of C. Aubrey Smith, the man who played Colonel Zap in my favorite swashbuckler, *The Prisoner of Zenda.* Yes, I would apply to go there with Bob. I notified the school secretary that I wanted to apply to Millbrook, then got permission to use the office telephone. I placed a person-to-person collect call to Mrs. Julia Szyk in New York.

Aunt Julia did come to my graduation dance. She told me that she had bought a new long dress just for the occasion and had her hair done. No one had ever done so much for me before, and I couldn't help feeling guilty over causing her the expense.

Her dress, I remember, was beige with large blue flowers. *One two with the left, one two with the right,* I counted, leading my aunt around the gym floor the way Miss Linda, who came every other Wednesday to teach us to dance, had instructed. Aunt Julia, who had danced on the stage of the Yiddish Theater in Poland, towered over me and followed.

The following morning, before the commencement service, was the traditional father/son baseball game. Arriving at Rumsey for the start of a new school year we had always looked forward to the appearance of some new boy named Charlie DiMaggio or Billy Williams, whose dad would come and pound the ball out of sight the morning of commencement, but it never happened.

I had just been elected captain of the baseball team, probably on the strength of the home run I had hit in some game with another school. Like my hero, Lou Gehrig, I played first base. We knew there would be no DiMaggio or Feller or Williams playing against us, only sweaty men in suit pants, street shoes, and white shirts, whose wives would urge them not to overdo. A few masters filled in.

"Pound one out of there, Padowicz!" the younger boys yelled as I stood at the plate, and, as I recall, I did get on base a couple of times, but we lost anyway. We had only won one game all term.

Aunt Julia was in the stands with no idea of what she was watching. A third former was explaining the game to her, and Aunt Julia listened intently. Later, I heard that when he had finished, the third former asked if she had understood, and Aunt Julia assured him that she had.

"So explain it back to me," the young man had said.

Aunt Julia said that instead she pulled a box of Chiclets from her bag and offered one to her instructor.

Then I saw Uncle Arthur sitting beside her. He had come that morning in his new Chevrolet (one of the first cars built since the beginning of the war) with his new chauffeur, a black man named Major.

After all the ceremonies I said good-bye to my two remaining classmates—for the summer. We had each applied to and been accepted by Millbrook and would be meeting again in the fall.

Then I climbed into my uncle and aunt's car, and Major drove us to their new house in New Canaan, Connecticut.

The house in New Canaan was huge. The two-story entry hall was large enough to play badminton in. Aunt and Uncle had a corner bedroom on the second floor. Cousin Alice, with her husband, Joe, their little girls, and the nanny occupied three more bedrooms on that floor. One bedroom was to be mine until Mother sent for me, and one was for Alice's brother, George, soon to be returning from the war with his French wife, Collette, and infant daughter.

The house sat on ten acres of land maintained by a man named Jimmy, who lived with his wife, Helen, and toddler son, Robert, in an apartment over the garage. Major doubled as a butler, and his wife and sister served as maids. Aunt Julia did her own cooking. The three servants lived on the third floor of the main house.

Aunt Julia and Uncle Arthur loved to entertain. Guests would come for the weekend, bringing their own friends. Uncle Arthur, who rose early and retired early, would say that he never knew what total strangers he might encounter at the breakfast table.

I had a summer job. I was to be assistant to Jimmy, the gardener, until Mother sent for me from Lima. My pay was five dollars a week. Five dollars a week did not buy very much even in those days, but I knew no one in New Canaan and had no way to spend my money.

Uncle Arthur had a room with a large window where he did his painting. When I got up at seven he was already at work, taking advantage of the morning light from the northern sky. As he had in New York, he worked in a small space on a huge desk covered with little bottles, brushes, paints, and pencils. He whistled as he worked, producing a clear sound, perfectly on pitch. The tune was always the same, Stephen Foster's "Beautiful Dreamer."

Uncle Arthur was a *Zionist*. What that meant, I was told, was that he was working to have Palestine declared a nation for Jews. My aunt explained to me that his caricatures, now that Hitler and Tojo were no longer around, were devoted mostly to something called *civil rights*. His celebrity as an artist brought him into contact with many important people whom he would bring together to build public opinion in favor of a free Jewish state. At the same time, his paintings depicting the injustice of prejudice and the preciousness of freedom influenced the general public. Virtually ignorant of world affairs, I did not recognize the names of the many political and cultural leaders who visited the New Canaan house. Later in life I would be told that I had met two future prime ministers of Israel, Golda Meir and Menachem Begin, poetry anthologist Louis Untermeyer, and actor Frederick March at the Szyks.

While Uncle Arthur claimed that I did not disturb him when I stood looking over his shoulder as he worked, we did not have much of a relationship. I enjoyed his wit at the dinner table, as much of it as I understood. But isolated as I was in boarding school for most of the year, I understood little of the political issues that concerned him. He never inquired into my state of affairs and I, of course, was not accustomed to bringing my problems to the attention of grownups.

I did, however, develop close relationships with Jimmy, the gardener, and Major, the butler/chauffeur. Jimmy shared his vast store of knowledge about Major League baseball with me as we worked around the grounds, and

Major let me steer the car. Back in Poland, when Kiki and I visited with my grandparents in Lodz, she and I would accompany Grandfather on his daily carriage rides to the park. Kiki would sit in back with Grandfather, and I would sit beside Adam, the coachman. When we reached the park, Adam would hand me the reins. Now, when we were alone in the Chevrolet, Major would let me sit beside him and handle the steering wheel.

My exposure to African Americans had been very limited. The cleaning woman that used to come to Mother's apartment did not seem much different from our domestic servants in Warsaw, and Mother seemed to treat her with the same respect. There were no black faces at Rumsey or in the Cornwall community, but in history class we learned about the cruelty of slavery and the prejudice that still existed in the minds and actions of our less-civilized Caucasian fellow citizens to the south. In the comfort of our all-white community, we learned to believe that "all men are created equal," and that Jim Crow was an abomination.

As my friendship with Major developed that summer, I could not help but feel a certain guilt for the accumulation of injustice that my adopted country had heaped upon Major's people. I constantly looked for ways that I could demonstrate to him my own total lack of prejudice.

The opportunity finally appeared with the much anticipated boxing match between the Negro Joe Louis, Heavyweight Champion of the World, and the Caucasian challenger, Billy Conn. In his last fight before enlisting in the army, Joe Louis had fought the wily Billy Conn, a highly skilled boxer who, according to the experts, had been ahead on points until he grew careless and had gotten himself knocked out. Now the world waited for a rematch.

The idea of dethroning Joe Louis, who had been champion of the world as long as I could remember, was as

absurd as that of Governor Dewey beating President Roosevelt a few years earlier. Louis, Roosevelt, and the New
York Yankees were institutions on which the stability of
the world was based. In my support for Joe Louis I saw an
opportunity to demonstrate my colorblindness to Major.
I asked him if I might listen to the fight with him in
their third-floor bedroom and was invited to do so. Major,
his wife, and I were joined in their sweltering room by
Major's twenty-something sister, who sat across from me
cross-legged on the bed in her bra and panties. I found
it difficult to concentrate on the fight, though I think I
showed sufficient enthusiasm for Louis's eventual victory.

One day Aunt Julia called me in from the lawn I was
mowing to talk with her in the library. She had just had
a telephone conversation with my mother. It appeared that
my going to Lima would not be possible in the immediate
future. When I pressed her for details, my aunt explained
that anti-Semitism, a reality of which we were particularly
aware, happened to be exceptionally strong in the circles
in which Mother and Pierre moved in Lima. I did not
understand what relevance this had. I knew Pierre was
Catholic and my peroxide-blonde mother had been equally
Catholic for some time now.

  Pierre's diplomatic career could well be jeopardized, my
aunt went on to explain, and I didn't want that to happen,
did I? I assured her that I did not, though I still had no
idea what that might have to do with me.

  "Well then, you'll just spend the rest of the summer
with us," Aunt Julia assured me.

  Suddenly I understood a great deal. Suddenly I understood the logic behind Mother's strange habit of explaining
that I had been hit in the nose by a croquet mallet on the
ship coming from Brazil whenever she introduced me to

one of her friends. Up to this moment, that this should be so essential an element of my identity had seemed as far-fetched as the idea of trying to play croquet onboard ship. Now I understood just how important my Sunday church attendance in school was to Mother, why I had spent so little of my vacation time in her company, and how I was, in fact, a walking advertisement for the inconvenient element of Mother's nature.

I spent the rest of the summer pushing a lawn mower around the property. In the fall, Major drove me to Millbrook School for Boys in Millbrook, New York.

Chapter Ten

There was a quiet air of academic professionalism at Millbrook. Here, contrary to my Rumsey experience, you had the sense that the masters were professional teachers rather than men ineligible for the draft. The buildings were brick except for the whitewashed barn and the silo that had been part of a farm fifteen years earlier. The student body of 120 boys was three times the size of Rumsey's.

The Millbrook senior class, I soon learned, did not have desks in the study hall but did their homework in their rooms. When the entire school assembled in the study hall for morning announcements and for Sunday worship services, the sixth formers sat on benches built into light oak paneling around the room. Into that paneling were carved, by class, the names of boys who had graduated. And the realization I soon made that, if I managed to graduate, my own name would be carved into that paneling as well totally blew my mind. It was only a remote possibility, since I expected the truth of my defective character to catch up to me at any time, but if I could hold it off for four more years, some craftsman would be engaged to come and carve the name *Julian Padowicz* into that bleached oak paneling along with the names of my classmates. There it would remain as a part of other people's lives for a long, long time, even while I rotted in a relative's attic. It was a recognition I had never anticipated. I counted four panels and knew exactly the one where my name would, some day, be located.

There were three football teams at Millbrook: varsity, junior varsity, and midgets. As one of the youngest boys, I tried out for a backfield position on the midgets and made it. Among my peers, I was greased lightning. At Rumsey, it had taken me and my Hebraic nose years to gain recognition for anything other than my many shortcomings, but now I had it for my football ability.

I wasn't the only running back of interest that season. The United States Military Academy at West Point, New York, was having quite a season as well, led by a tandem duo referred to as *Mr. Inside* and *Mr. Outside*, Cadets Felix "Doc" Blanchard and Glenn Davis, respectively. My hero was my fellow fullback, Doc Blanchard, who steamed through opposing players like a hot knife through butter.

The University of Notre Dame was having a fine season as well, led by quarterback Johnny Lujack. On November 9, these two football powers met at Yankee Stadium in a regular season game that all acknowledged would determine the heavyweight championship of American football.

We were playing a game of our own that afternoon, and I could not listen to the radio broadcast. I don't remember whom we played or whether we won or lost. But I did learn afterward that the two titans battled to a nothing/nothing tie with Mr. Lujack stopping my hero, Doc Blanchard from scoring the winning touchdown by a last minute tackle, a tackle he would never have made had Cadet Blanchard not had an injured knee.

I was assigned a single room at first. I didn't like living alone. At night, instead of the clandestine whispering as at

Rumsey, my new greased-lightning persona fell away and I was left to confront my own devils. And devils they were.

That I read slowly was an unfortunate characteristic, possibly accountable to my learning to read at an advanced age. But the fact that I allowed my mind to wander from the printed word and dwell on my exploits on the gridiron, scenes from a movie I had recently seen, or the anatomical features of one of the masters' wives was undeniably the fault of my crummy character. The masters and boys here at Millbrook, who smiled at me and addressed me as "Paddy," a nickname I had somehow acquired, didn't know that behind my friendly banter and eagerness to please there lived black-souled, deceitful "Julian." A boy who didn't care enough to concentrate his thoughts where they should be concentrated, gave deceitful opinions on homework assignments he had not really read, and had not once made the Rumsey Effort List after his first year. What kept me from easing my pain with tears was the shameful image of little Julian whimpering under his blanket at Rumsey.

That I was placed in the lowest section of each course that I took did not inspire me to earn promotion to a higher one. I thanked my lucky stars still to be included in any active school program. In the dark moments of my lonely nights, I recalled the image Mother's friend, Mr. Michael, had planted in my mind of life as a failure in a relative's attic. Oh, I would write stories in that attic, applying my talent for assembling words and for plot development, but their content would be the content of schoolboy fantasies of football, fighting Japs in the Pacific, and faculty wives removing their clothes. The life experiences of an Ernest Hemingway, a John Steinbeck, or a Damon Runyon would never be mine. Fortunately, unlike Rumsey's troublemaking Effort List, Millbrook did

not attempt to report to parents how hard their sons were
trying on a weekly basis.

I didn't know what to expect in the way of Christmas at the
home of my Zionist uncle. What I discovered was that my
Aunt Julia, the former Yiddish theater actress who spoke
every language with an almost comic Yiddish accent and
who pronounced the holiday as "*Hrismes*," had as much
of the Christmas spirit as anyone I'd known. A tree in the
entrance hall reached to the second-floor ceiling. Under
the tree, a separate pile of gifts for each member of the
household, including servants, contained one gift-wrapped
parcel from each member of the family.

Particularly memorable was the Christmas of 1947. It
had begun snowing several days before Christmas, and it
wouldn't let up. The driveway was, maybe, a hundred yards
long with an upward incline at the entrance and guests
would be coming. The family turned out in boots and mit-
tens, brandishing shovels of various descriptions. Only my
uncle, who had suffered a heart attack a few years earlier,
was excused from driveway shoveling.

Back from Lima and staying in Mother's New York
apartment were my mother and Pierre. Pierre had just been
appointed vice consul to Montreal, Canada. But Mother's
East Sixty-Third Street apartment was rent controlled. This
meant that the landlord could not raise the rent, and this
rent was set at what soon became a ridiculously low level.
Mother would keep this apartment for the rest of her life
as a pied-à-terre that she "could not afford to let go."

On Christmas Eve, my mother and Pierre were due to
arrive by train sometime in the afternoon, but the road
to the station, some two miles away, was not plowed.
Or it had been plowed and covered again. At any rate,
there was more than a foot of snow on the road and no

chance to pick them up by car. And Pierre, with his artificial leg that reached practically to his hip, didn't stand
a chance. So Alice's husband, Joe; her brother, George,
now back from the war; and I dragged an American Flyer
sled, borrowed from Jimmy's son, to the New Canaan
station. There, we loaded the French vice consul onto
the American Flyer, told my mother that, regrettably,
she had to walk, three-inch heels and all, and set off for
the Szyks'.

A week after Christmas comes New Year's, and the Szyks
had planned a party of several dozen people. With our
Polish background, the default beverage of the house was
vodka, which is best drunk chilled. And the snow banks
along the shoveled footpath to the front door provided an
ideal refrigerator for the several cases of vodka procured
for the occasion. Soon the protruding red tops of vodka
bottles adorned our path to the front door.

Then, on New Year's Eve, it snowed again. While our
shovel brigade fought valiantly to keep the driveway open,
the vodka bottles along the patio became covered. Ine-
briated gentlemen in shirtsleeves, suspenders, and black
bowties could be seen thrusting their arms deep into snow
banks for hours into 1948.

The story of my parents' early return from Peru could
be told two ways. Mother's version was, "Oh, they loved
Pierre so much that they promoted him to vice consul for
Montreal." The version that I would hear some years later
from reliable sources was that the French ambassador's wife
had requested that Paris remove the troublesome Mme.
Gabard from her husband's domain. And, as a highly decorated, heavily wounded companion-at-arms of Free France's
leader, Pierre was reassigned to the consulate in Montreal,
where his Polish wife might be less likely to make waves.

When I first heard of their return earlier that Christmas vacation, I took the train to New York the following morning at Mother's invitation for a day visit of "a movie and ice cream." While I was still a great fan of both movies and ice cream, and remain so to this day, then in my early teens I resented the implication that my attention could be bought, or needed to be bought, in this way. I had a genuine desire to see my mother and her sympathetic husband that was not being acknowledged. I did not arrive at Grand Central in a good humor.

I walked to East Sixty-Third Street and arrived at Mother's fifth floor apartment. "Oh, you've grown so big, Julian," Mother said, leaning forward and offering her cheek. Whether she was referring to all of me or just my nose, I wasn't sure. I made the obligatory kissing sound.

"Kiss Pierre," she said sotto voce in Polish, as her husband caned his way into the living room. I shook his hand, instead. It was not the warm greeting I wanted to give him. I liked the man, and I wasn't sure I had done him any favors by selecting him over Reggie, but I was not going to be told how to greet him by my mother. And I most certainly wasn't going to kiss him.

Mother had smoked salmon and cream cheese sandwiches for our lunch, which we ate off our laps in the living room, there being no dining facility in the little apartment.

During lunch, Mother told me how bored I would have been visiting in Lima. There was no baseball and everyone spoke either Spanish or French. That I had not been invited to visit Lima did not bother me, and the implications behind the real reason I had not been invited did not really affect me. That I was a burden to my mother—one that she so heroically shouldered—had been pointed out to me by many of her friends and relatives, and it did not enter my mind that I should be seen as anything else. Had I had more exposure to the family life of other boys I would not have been so tolerant.

Asked to choose a movie, I could have selected some Abbott and Costello–like comedy, which Pierre and I would enjoy and Mother would hate, but I found more satisfaction in choosing one that both my parents would enjoy. We saw something with Greer Garson or Claudette Colbert, and I enjoyed the fact that Mother and Pierre got to enjoy a movie that I had selected.

That Mother seemed to have forgotten about the ice cream part of the visit was all right with me. It seemed that they had a very important cocktail party to attend, so they dropped me off at Grand Central with a twenty dollar bill.

Chapter Eleven

Thanksgiving at the Szyks was as spirited as Christmas, though I doubt that my aunt knew exactly what we were celebrating. A couple days after our turkey feast during my second year at Millbrook, my aunt invited me to join them on a social visit. "Vy don't you come vit us," she said. "Dere is a girl your aitch."

My heart immediately began to beat faster—not from lust, but from terror. I had never been in the company of a strange girl before. In Rio, when I was eight, I had been infatuated with a beautiful woman in her twenties whom Mother had engaged to take me to the beach, but other than Ann Marr and my cousin Anita, I had never as much as spoken to a female anywhere near my own age.

Aunt and Uncle's friends were a family named Davidoff who lived a ten-minute ride away. Dr. Leo Davidoff, it turned out, was a renowned neurosurgeon, and there were three daughters and a son. The girl who was my age was the middle daughter, named Leonore. The boy, Frank, was a year or so younger.

There was music coming from somewhere when Dr. Davidoff met us at the door, and it stopped as we entered the living room. The girl he introduced to me as Leonore had been playing a flute, if I remember correctly, while her younger sister, Mary Libby, played a cello and their mother, the piano. There was a fire in the fireplace. Frank was playing backgammon across the room with Leonore's best friend. Out of concern for her privacy, I will call her Susan.

I have no memory of what we talked about. I can't imagine that I had anything to talk about other than boarding school life. But Leonore seemed very interested in what I had to say. And when she toasted a marshmallow in the fireplace, blew on it with her own breath, and gave it to me to eat, I was smitten.

Leonore was my height with straight, shoulder-length dark hair and dark eyes. In her presence, I never ran out of things to say, and she met everything I said with either a thoughtful response or the most beautiful laugh I had ever heard. Her older sister, Helen, and Mary Libby were courteous to me as well. In fact, the entire family seemed interested in me and my life in boarding school.

It was soon evident to me that the Davidoff family had been alerted to this teenage boy who knew no one in New Canaan and whose mother had sloughed him off on relatives because she had no room for him in her life. While I was not aware of actually suffering any pain due to this condition I knew how it might tug at one's heartstrings, and this caring family was clearly responding.

I was invited to come back the following day but unfortunately my vacation was over and I would be heading back to Millbrook. "Then we must get together when you come home for Christmas," Leonore said. "You are coming to New Canaan, aren't you?"

I now had a roommate at Millbrook, a boy named David Chandler, who was a great deal smarter than I was but not as athletic. In fact, he wasn't even a little athletic. To see him standing on the practice field in football pads and helmet, you knew immediately that this was not going to work. I was far from the best athlete in school, or even in my class, but my speed made me successful enough to give me a sense of identity. David, on the other hand, read and discussed writers and poets I couldn't understand and knew about such things as fine art and jazz.

David asked me to teach him to catch a baseball, and I tried. But he proved even more inept than Jules's sister, Ann. I laughed at David's clumsiness, and he smiled at my cultural ignorance. We were good friends and well matched in accomplishment.

That was, until we returned from the Thanksgiving vacation and I told him that I had a girlfriend. David did not have a girlfriend and, I judged by his self-consciousness, would not be capable of acquiring one on his own. I told him that I would invite Leonore to the school dance during the winter term, and that she had a best friend named Susan whom he might invite as well. I told him that during Christmas vacation I would get Susan's address for him.

Arriving at the Szyks' for Christmas vacation, my first order of business was to telephone Leonore to let her know I was back—and hope for an invitation. She said to come over the next day.

The following morning there was snow on the ground, and my first duty was to help in digging out our own driveway. It was noon before I was released, and I hiked the two miles or so to the Davidoffs, a shovel over my shoulder, with the hope that my services might be of use there.

As a surgeon, Dr. Davidoff was not supposed to handle things like shovels, which left twelve- or thirteen-year-old Frank as the only male available to shovel snow. Much to my delight, I found their driveway—though considerably shorter than ours—only half shoveled, while Frank struggled mightily with the only shovel the family owned. Like a cowboy arriving at a wagon train under siege by Indians, I pitched right in, without a word, and soon Frank and I had the driveway dug out. Leonore and her family were grateful.

Within a couple of days I realized, much to my surprise, that what I had told David had been the truth. I did, indeed, have a girlfriend. I wasn't just a boy whom Leonore knew, but her *boyfriend*. We sledded together on a nearby hill, skated on a neighbor's pond—where I found myself the best skater there—and went to the movies together. Then Leonore invited me to be her escort at a formal dance at a local country club.

I did not own a tuxedo, but my aunt informed me that my blue suit with Uncle's black bow tie would be just fine. That just left the dancing. Here, Aunt Julia leveled with me. While our evening together at my Rumsey graduation had been "delightful," the terpsichorean technique I had exhibited at that time would not do for Leonore. Now Aunt Julia took it upon herself to teach me proper ballroom dancing. We rolled up the Oriental rug in the big entrance hall and danced to the music of Bing Crosby, the Andrews Sisters, and the new kid, Frank Sinatra. Aunt Julia, a large woman to begin with, had a large bosom as well, making it a little awkward for my fourteen-year-old arms, but we braved through the difficulty, and Leonore found herself squired by a master of the foxtrot and the waltz.

Of course I knew that none of this would last. While I followed Mother's admonition to smile and tell funny stories, I was sure that Leonore would soon discover what a sad person I really was. When she wrote to tell me that she could not come to Millbrook's Winter Dance Weekend, I took this as the subtle beginning of the end of our relationship and was duly heartbroken—even though I had known from the outset that it would all end badly.

In the absence of official notification I continued writing letters, never mentioning my broken heart but causing myself further misery by pretending that I had sensed nothing. Of course I was an old hand at grief. Kiki, my beloved nanny and the only mother figure I had known, had painfully disappeared from my life without warning when I was seven, and numerous times I had come to believe that, in her own peculiar way, Mother did approve of me only to have that belief painfully dashed each time. But the loss of Leonore's good opinion (I had not dared dream in the realms of *affection*) had a different and even more poignant flavor.

When I came home for spring vacation and made my obligatory telephone call to Leonore, I discovered that my conclusion had been totally wrong. I was invited to come as soon as possible to listen to Leonore and her siblings play classical music, after which we could toast marshmallows and even get away for a walk.

While I wasn't crazy about marshmallows generally, Leonore's blowing on one seemed to endow it with a special flavor, and I became aware of a strong desire to run my tongue around the inside of Leonore's mouth.

I had never heard of a person performing such oral acrobatics. When I saw men and women kissing on the screen, I saw the pressing together of closed lips, which had its attraction as well, but not to the degree that the interior of Leonore's mouth seemed to offer. I took this to be some aberrant product of my perverted brain and endeavored to maintain a prudent distance between our faces at all times.

Supplied with movie money by Aunt Julia, I took Leonore to the local theater, where I dearly longed to hold her sweet hand. But I didn't know if this was acceptable by the rules of behavior for people our age. I could not bear the embarrassment of outraging Leonore's sensibilities and kept my hands to myself.

It wasn't till the middle of summer vacation that the anticipated shoe finally landed. I do not say *second shoe* because there had been no first one—only my foreboding of impending rejection. For no reason I knew of, but plenty that I could imagine, Leonore informed me that she no longer wanted me as her boyfriend. She gave me back my ID bracelet, and I returned hers. We parted as friends.

Some days later, when I had gotten over my heartbreak, I telephoned the only other nonrelated girl I knew (except for Ann Marr, who was not around and whom I did not regard as a dating concept). That was Leonore's best friend, the large-eyed, olive-skinned Susan. I invited her to the movies.

Susan had to check with Leonore before responding and, eventually, accepted. We saw a Technicolor swashbuckler about a pirate, I think starring Gene Kelly.

I got my driver's license that summer, and I would walk some forty-five minutes to Susan's house, drive to the movies and back in her parents' old Packard, then hike home. A few times I got the use of the Szyks' car. The problem, though, was that Susan had to be home by eleven o'clock, often forcing us to leave the theater before the movie ended.

Susan's family lived on a windy, hilly street on the other side of town. It was a property that her father's parents, peasants from Italy, had bought when they first arrived in America and where they proceeded to grow grapes and, maybe, onions. Figuratively, in prosperous New Canaan this was on the other side of the tracks.

The farmer grandparents were both deceased at this point. Susan's father had suffered what was called *shell shock* in the First World War, in which he had served as a motorcycle courier, and now had a temperament that did not permit him to hold a job. Receiving a disability pension and not interested in agriculture, he had cut down the vineyard and, in its place, built a rental house with his own hands. Now he maintained the property, cooked the meals, and spent spare time at a local bar with his best friend, a terrier named Tippy.

Susan's mother was the recognized breadwinner, operating a shop that she and her sister-in-law had started during the Great Depression and made into a modest but thriving business. There were ten years between Susan and her older sister. Their father had suffered a breakdown on his honeymoon, after the sister was conceived, and spent the next ten years in the Veterans Administration Hospital. It was during that period that Susan's mother and her sister-in-law had opened their shop.

Susan's family was clearly not of the same socioeconomic class as the Davidoffs and my own relatives. It is only in retrospect that I realize what the small rooms of their modest house, the subject of their conversations, and the general style of their life reminded me of most. It was the times that my Polish nanny, Kiki, had taken me to visit her own father in Lodz. Unlike the chatter that prevailed in the Szyk or the Davidoff households, there was a prevailing silence in Susan's house that mirrored that in the home of Kiki's widowed father.

Or perhaps I should call it a hollow, or a lack of resonance. It was explained to me that some years earlier Susan's emotionally challenged father had perpetrated some act which had "killed" his wife's love for him, and so, during waking hours his movements about the house were limited to the kitchen, where he cooked, and the dining room with its television. Susan's mother entertained Susan and me, as well as her Italian American friends, by herself in the small living room. Her own parents having come from a part of Italy north of that from which her peasant in-laws came, Susan's mother maintained a definite condescension toward those friends from more southerly parts of that country.

To my mind Susan and her family were connected to my beloved Kiki and hers. And to me, Kiki's family were the standard to which all others were compared. Economic prosperity and intellectual sophistication above that standard were suspect. Nor did it escape my awareness that, like Kiki and her family, Susan and hers were Catholic. So here, on the other side of New Canaan's tracks, I had found my lost Kiki.

A student in good standing at New Canaan's fine high school and the best friend of Leonore Davidoff, Susan had the social skills to be acceptable at the Szyks' dinner table, where she now became a frequent visitor. But I knew Mother would not be altogether pleased by this liaison, and I found particular pleasure in this thought. That my affections should be directed toward this lower-middle-class family was, I felt, the loudest, most affirmative statement I had ever made.

But all this was only the second, supporting reason for my affection for Susan. The primary reason was that this attractive, popular high school girl was willing to call me her boyfriend. For some reason, with Susan the feeling of being unworthy of her affections and in constant danger of being discovered and discarded was less than it had been with Leonore. For reasons I could not imagine, Susan appeared to be totally accepting of my attentions.

Just as attractive, in my judgment, as Leonore, Susan played a clarinet in the New Canaan High School Band. Catholic, she did not have Leonore's passion for politics pertaining to the fledgling state of Israel, which was fine with me. Her musical taste, like my own, was popular rather than classical. We sang songs together, rather than my listening to her play the flute, though Susan found my ability to carry a tune somewhat substandard.

And Susan was extremely athletic. In fact, it was known around town that Susan was the best girl athlete New Canaan High had ever had, surpassing even her older sister. Susan was someone I could play tennis with. When we danced, I could feel the muscles of her back.

Susan had another characteristic that distinguished her from Leonore. At the Szyks' dinner table, my uncle would usually express his opinions and feelings about world affairs in a humorous vein. Humor was his weapon of choice. Whether he spoke of the now-defeated Nazis, the anti-Israel Arabs, or Republicans, as he did with his art my uncle always managed to find an interpretation of their stance that made them vulnerable to ridicule. And those of us at the table, just like the millions who enjoyed his caricatures, would dissolve in laughter.

And here, I had unconsciously found a father image and arrived at the belief that making people laugh was a good way to win their affection. I had put this to work when I was with Leonore, and found her appreciative when I quoted my uncle's humor and nearly as appreciative when I made humorous comments of my own. In fact, in Leonore's presence I had made the realization that I had the capacity, occasionally, to originate a truly humorous statement. Susan, on the other hand, never found either my humor, or that of my uncle, to be funny. Making fun of people, she informed me, particularly people who were not there to defend themselves, was abusive and unkind.

I could not argue with this. While not as intellectual as Leonore, Susan, I came to believe, was a considerably more moral person—another resemblance to my sainted Kiki. That she would not allow herself to be carried away by even my uncle's professional humor I came to consider a great strength. And at the base of this, there still lay the fact that my brain was an undisciplined mess and, if images of myself living out my life in a relative's attic no longer haunted me the way they had before, there was no denying that I still considered myself not as worthy of appreciation or affection as other people. Even though I was no longer pudgy and could hold my own on an athletic field, even though I understood perfectly well the necessity for Kiki's returning to her own family at the outbreak of war, at bottom, I was still that twice-rejected spawn, that embarrassment to his mother and usurper of educational services with his unfortunate nose who was even now lying to Susan about having been baptized into the Catholic faith by a Polish priest in Barcelona.

Susan did come to the next Millbrook dance weekend and several more after that. She did, however, find the whole idea of a school where rich people sent their sons at great expense to mix only with their own kind to be laughable, particularly when excellent schools like New Canaan High were available for free and where kids from all socioeconomic backgrounds rubbed shoulders and were judged on their individual merit. When she said that the money would be better spent feeding the hungry in China and India, I could do little but hang my head in shame. And when she told me how proud she was that her achievements were all her own, in contrast to my spoon-fed existence, I was learning how small and artificial my world really was.

I wrote to her every day and received one or two letters a week in return. I gave her my Millbrook jacket, my ID bracelet, and my yachting cap and received a box of scallop-edged stationery at Christmas. While on the surface all this did not seem terribly fair, I knew that my knowledge of boyfriend/girlfriend etiquette was as nonexistent as my knowledge of most things pertaining to interpersonal relationships. I trusted the well-rounded, popular, and socially conscious Susan to set the rules and was grateful that she continued her association with me despite my inadequacies.

On the subject of church attendance, Millbrook also had its small group of Catholic boys who had to be driven to mass in town every Sunday. Unlike Rumsey, however, Millbrook had a master, Mr. Prum, who was also Catholic and drove us. Xavier Prum was a jolly, Santa Claus–like physics teacher who came from Luxemburg, spoke with a heavy accent, and was rumored to have served as prime minister of that little country, as well as to have worked with Albert Einstein.

Like Father Sullivan, Mr. Prum soon became concerned over my never taking communion, and would, occasionally, take me aside to tell me what damage I was doing to my immortal soul by this abstinence. Realizing that my former explanation of coming from a long line of priests and waiting for my uncle to come from Poland to give me my first communion would no longer fly, I would just hang my head in shame.

I felt really bad about having to lie to Mr. Prum, who was clearly concerned about my well-being. And I was lying to my roommate, Dave, who also happened to be Catholic, and I didn't like that either. On the other hand, attending mass with Dave was more enjoyable than it had been at Rumsey. On several occasions we managed to sit behind two girls our age, and when we saw the one in front of Dave slip her shoe off while she knelt, I had Dave convinced that it was a signal she was sending to him.

In those days, the Catholic Church would rate films for "decency," and every so often the priest would tell us from the pulpit about a film that had just been released and had been judged unsuitable for Catholic sensibilities. He would then have us all raise our right hand and swear that we would not go see it. One such Sunday, Dave nudged me to point out that Mr. Prum appeared to be the only person in church who had not raised his hand but stood with both hands planted firmly on the back of the pew in front of him. The physics teacher immediately went up a notch in our esteem.

My mother and Pierre, in the meantime, had settled in Montreal, where they rented a small apartment on Pierre's modest salary. However, Mother's old friend—the wealthy, important, and highly mobile Reggie Purbrick—remained a fixture in their lives, and their humble lifestyle seemed to reflect a periodic influx of cash. What exactly the arrangement was, I never asked. On the other hand, I was old enough now to imagine several scenarios that were both titillating and embarrassing.

I would visit them for a week or so at a time. There was little for me to do in Montreal, and I didn't like being separated from Susan when I was on vacation. I wasn't sure what I might come back to.

Mother tried remedying that situation. She never said that she disapproved of Susan, but I knew that with Susan's lower-middle-class background and her disdain for Mother's values, she could not be Mother's first choice for a

prospective daughter-in-law. The super in Mother's building had a daughter my age, and Mother thought that I
should meet her. One day, Mother and I met the super's
wife on the stairs, as she was cleaning them, and Mother
proceeded to ask her to bring her daughter around that
evening so that I could take her to a movie. I was mortified beyond measure.

Being mortified by Mother was not a new experience.
Standing beside her on a street in occupied Poland as she
negotiated with a woman in line outside a butcher shop to
be let in while the people behind her howled their protests
had been bad enough. There, I had been only an append-
age. Here, having Mother negotiate this way for my supposed pleasure was more than I could stand. I abandoned
Mother on the stairs and rushed for the apartment. When
the super's daughter knocked on our door after supper, I
would not come out of my room.

On one of my visits I noticed that Mother looked strangely
different. I thought that maybe she had lost weight. Women
were always talking about losing weight, and while I didn't
think Mother had any to lose, she was always careful not
to consume starchy food. But after a while I realized what
it was. What was different was her nose. Mother's straight
nose, I realized, had suddenly become shorter and now
turned up. I knew about plastic surgery and nose jobs
and understood what had happened without having to ask
questions. What I wasn't prepared for, however, was when
Mother sat me down and announced that I was going to
have my nose shortened and turned up as well.

Disagreements between Mother and me were nothing
new. On the other hand, defying her outright had never
been a part of my situation. This time, however, I gave her
a very definite *no. No, Ma'am! No way, Jose! Niet!*

To my great surprise, I now found myself in a negotiation. I was offered two thousand dollars for the objectionable half inch of nose. Money was not a big issue with me. Spending most of my time in boarding school, I had little need for money. My response remained negative.

Then Mother's tactic changed. "You could be a very handsome man," she said. "Your nose keeps people from seeing your face. It's all they see."

My nose was all that Mother saw. The issue, I knew, wasn't making me look handsome. The issue was getting the *Jew* out of *Julian*. But my objection wasn't ethnic. It was just that somehow my psyche saw this as a line beyond which my mother could not cross into my life.

For Christmas that year I received a typewriter from Mother and Pierre, a gray Royal portable machine in a tan case. I would not travel without it. In my spare time, I would sit at that typewriter and write short stories. Ring Lardner, O. Henry, and Damon Runyon were my heroes, and the irony of a twist ending irresistible. I also admired the gentle humor of Mr. Runyon, but did not attempt to replicate it.

I wrote one story about a young couple who go to visit a famous satirist at his home in Vermont. The man is lionized for writing stories about animals that talk, as in Orwell's *Animal Farm*, and through them laying bare the foibles of humanity. Except that the young couple discover that the famous man has no opinions on the foibles of humanity—he is simply writing about talking sheep and talking chickens. Another was about a gentle old college professor who is visited in his garden by a beautiful woman. She charms him into accompanying her and turns out to be Death coming to claim him in the same gentle way that he has lived his life.

These stories I would immediately send to *The New Yorker*. I was pretty sure that *The New Yorker* would not be interested in them, but they sent rejection slips within ten days. Then I would send the story to the *Saturday Evening Post*, where I felt it might actually have a chance. By the time the *Post*'s rejection arrived, some six weeks later, I was usually into another story. The rejection slips I would tape to the wall of my Millbrook dorm room as an expression of my defiance of adversity.

In the back of my mind I remembered reading somewhere that to sell short stories you had to study the requirements of a given magazine and write your story to those specifications. But crafting a story that met magazine specifications was not something I could or was willing to do. It was my hope against hope that the *Saturday Evening Post* would see some genius in one of my stories that would make them toss out their silly parameters and publish my story on the basis of its own merits.

That this did not happen disappointed but did not discourage me. Writing a story was an immensely satisfying creative act and the most consistent satisfaction in my life. When my hero won out over adversity or saw the light of truth, I shared in that triumph. In addition, the fact that I had crafted an original story, complete with opening, development, and conclusion—even if no magazine wanted to print it—was achievement akin to flying the first heavier-than-air airplane. Had there been someone to read and respond to them—Susan liked dog stories—my satisfaction would have surpassed that of the Wright brothers.

Mother called me one day at Millbrook to say that she and Pierre would be coming to visit. She said to invite a friend to go to lunch with us. Remembering my Rumsey experience, I thought it wiser not to take that risk. I waited for them alone, seated on the "fire station" in the middle of the quadrangle. The fire station was a little shed housing numerous lengths of hose beside a multiple-headed fire hydrant.

A maroon Buick did show up on time, at ten thirty. Pierre, in his beret, beamed happily at the wheel. This car was the first model in which General Motors offered Dynaflow, Buick's first automatic transmission, and Pierre could operate it with his one foot. The pleasure I saw expressed on his round face made me very glad for him.

Before going to lunch, Mother wanted to meet my headmaster, Mr. Pulling. After I had made the introduction, the three of them huddled for half an hour in Mr. Pulling's study while I again waited at the fire station.

Then, at lunch, I learned two lessons. This being Sunday, New York law prohibited the sale of alcohol before a certain hour, and Pierre was very disappointed not to have his customary, analgesic, very light Scotch and soda. When he registered his disappointment to the waitress she summoned the owner, who soon appeared with the requested elixir. "The law says that I am not allowed to sell alcohol this morning," she explained, "but that doesn't mean I can't *give* it to my friends."

Pierre thanked his new friend, shook her hand, and passed some money into her palm. At this point Mother proceeded to explain to her that Pierre was the vice consul of France in Montreal and that she, herself, had written a book some six years earlier recounting her escape from Bolshevik occupation of eastern Poland, namely a fourteen-hour (up from eleven) trek over the Carpathian Mountains. As I clearly remember, the implication this time was that she had made the journey alone. The lady owner was duly impressed, and Pierre handed her another bill.

The second lesson I learned had to do with their talk with my headmaster. Mr. Pulling had, apparently, had nice things to say about my personality. According to him, I was a very sympathetic boy, which pleased me, I think, more than it did Mother. But what really disappointed her was what he said about my roommate, David. David, he had said, was the kind of boy whom you could leave in a library and he would educate himself. What displeased Mother was the fact that this had not been said about me. "Yulian," she said in Polish, while Pierre occupied himself with his Scotch, "I want you to be the kind of person about whom people say, 'He could be left in a library and he would educate himself.'"

Suddenly I realized that now I had a new unreachable standard to answer to and that Mother had absolutely no idea how people operated. On the other hand, living up to Mother's new expectation did not prove to be the problem I feared. I discovered that she had found her own solution some months later, when I heard her say to Mrs. Skouras, wife of the president of Twentieth Century-Fox, "Ze hedmahster of Julian's school told me zat Julian is ze kind of boy zat you can leave in a library, and he will educate himself."

I would hear this said about "Julian" many times after that and never again did I hear any concern on Mother's part over my actual performance. I soon realized that I had been replaced in Mother's mind by another Julian who resembled me less and less with each accounting.

I'm not sure exactly when my grandmother arrived. Grandmother had spent the war in occupied Poland. Either Pierre's or Reggie's government connections had gotten her released from Poland's Communist regime, and she was now in Montreal.

Of Russian origin, Grandmother spoke Russian, Polish, and German. Pierre spoke only French and English. Though in precarious health after her occupation ordeal, Grandmother loved to laugh. With the few words she picked up of French and English, gestures, and a lot of laughter, Grandmother had no trouble making herself understood. Her favorite occupation was playing gin rummy with Pierre, which he seemed to enjoy as much as she.

During a short stay in New York, my mother introduced Grandmother to one of her friends, the actor Richard Ney. The handsome Mr. Ney was the former husband of actress Greer Garson, whose son he had played in the wartime film *Mrs. Miniver*. On Wednesday afternoons, Richard Ney—four years younger than my mother and speaking no more of Grandmother's languages than did Pierre—would pick her up in his Jaguar for a ride around Central Park. This they would follow with tea at the Plaza Hotel. When he delivered her back to Mother's Sixty-Third Street apartment, they would both be laughing and pronounce themselves to have had a marvelous time. In a private conversation some time later, Mr. Ney would tell me what a wonderful capacity my grandmother had for making you feel as though you were the most important person in her life.

Suffering from high blood pressure and looking considerably older than her fifty-some years, Grandmother eventually came to stay with the Szyks in New Canaan. Her sister's son, Uncle Arthur, was Grandmother's favorite nephew. This time there was no language barrier and what resulted was the wittiest repartee I have ever heard. Grandmother's wit turned out to be every bit as sharp as her nephew's, and when they went to work on some subject those of us who understood Polish were in for a treat.

Unfortunately I cannot remember any examples of that repartee except that when she first arrived and Uncle Arthur declared his house to be half hers, she asked how much he would pay her to sell her half back to him. When I asked her once whether she ever prayed, my frail grandmother answered that she didn't want to remind God that she was still down here.

Grandmother got on beautifully with my Susan. Whether she actually liked Susan or not I never knew, but she certainly made her feel as though she did. Having learned a few words of English by then, Grandmother mortified me now by addressing my olive-toned girlfriend as "My black girl." Advised by Aunt Julia that in America those words carried unintended implications, Grandmother would wave my aunt away, repeat the phrase, then proceed to present Susan with a bracelet or a scarf.

The Szyks had a television set in the library, a room lined with bookshelves my unliterary aunt had filled buying books by the yard on New York's Third Avenue—a street full of secondhand stores tucked under the El, the overhead rail line that lent itself so well to moviemakers for staging car chases and to indicate less desirable real estate. Most of the day, Grandmother watched wrestling on that television. Wrestling was plentiful programming in those days, and you could find it on one channel or another most times of the day or evening. Wrestling presented Grandmother with few language problems. She came to know the stars of the sport and the holds they were likely to apply in a given situation. There were Gene Stanlee, a silver-haired bodybuilder who, apparently, had held the title of Mr. America at one time and Antonino "Argentino" Rocca, a handsome newcomer who fought in his bare feet and could, at any moment, perform a cartwheel and grab his opponent around the neck with his legs. The names of others I don't remember.

Seated in her rocking chair in front of the snowy little screen, Grandmother would explain to me in her mixture of Polish and Russian what hold each contender would apply next. Since these were not real wrestling matches but choreographed ballets performed by entertainers with only rudimentary wrestling skills, their selection of holds and grips was limited, and Grandmother took pride in the accuracy of her prognostication. I tried, on one or two occasions, to clue Grandmother in to the showbiz nature of the sport, but she wouldn't hear of it.

Chapter Twelve

My old Rumsey roommate Rod Hodgins became editor of Millbrook's school paper, the *Silo*. Rod's recently retired father, Eric Hodgins, had been publisher of *Fortune* magazine. The reason for his retirement was a bit of good luck that had recently come his way.

When Rod and I were still at Rumsey, Mr. and Mrs. Hodgins, New Yorkers, had decided to move from the city to the country. They had bought a picturesque old house in New Milford, Connecticut, which they planned to have restored for their occupancy. But the restoration became a nightmare as the two city dwellers tried to cope with the mysteries of building construction and country living.

When the job was finally finished, far later than expected and at a far greater cost than estimated, Mr. Hodgins sat down at his typewriter and wrote a book about it. The book was called *Mr. Blandings Builds His Dream House* and proved an immediate best seller. Hollywood turned it into a film, and to this day, Cary Grant and Myrna Loy show up on television channels as Mr. and Mrs. Blandings.

For Rod to follow his father into journalism was a most reasonable step, and the editorship of the *Silo* was placed in his willing hands. Rod, in turn, appointed me to the post of reporter, and suddenly I found myself writing for publication.

While my writing until now had been a matter of thinking up an idea for a story, and then shaping it, now all I had to do was find out the facts and write them down in newspaper style. Rod explained newspaper inverted pyramid style and the four *W*s to me and I suddenly discovered how easy newspaper writing was. The arrival of a new faculty member, a new painting in the library, the birth of rabbits in the school's zoo, the school's chauffeur developing an instant coffeemaker all became grist for my mill. All I had to do was find out the facts and dress them up in clever words, as I had known how to do since Rumsey, and I had something to present proudly to Rod for publication. But, more than that, I now had a profession that I could take up after college.

Quite unique for a secondary school, Millbrook had an honest-to-goodness zoo. A biology teacher named Frank Trevor had joined the faculty early in the school's history in the 1930s and arrived with several small animals in the back of his car. With these as a start, he had built a zoo of small animals that was operated by the students. I don't remember what all we had. I know we had rabbits because I was in charge of them—and my charge was growing by the month. I remember we had a female South American kinkajou, a soft-furred little animal with a prehensile tail and an unpredictable disposition. Mr. Trevor explained that female kinkajous were often emotionally unstable.

We had a red-tailed hawk named Sister who ended up in the *Guinness Book of World Records* as the longest living red-tailed hawk on record. We had banks of tropical fish tanks. We had an official bird-banding station. That I didn't think of myself as living in some sort of boys' paradise is further proof that my head wasn't screwed on right.

As my Millbrook career progressed, I began finding myself no longer one of the bigger boys in my class. While I could still score touchdowns on the junior varsity, Mr. Kneutson, coach of the varsity onto which my larger classmates had already graduated, showed no interest in my abilities. This was a great disappointment to me, but I was no novice to disappointments. I did make the varsity in hockey, though I did not distinguish myself.

Baseball I found boring. Unless you're a pitcher or a catcher, I decided, you spend most of your time waiting for something to come your way and cheering someone else on. I did pitch a little on the midget team, but I wasn't very good at it.

In my sophomore year, Millbrook fielded a track team for the first time. Track presented a new alternative to baseball. I decided that the following spring I would switch to track.

When the spring term of my junior year came around, I reported for track practice. I was not interested in distance running but I discovered that with several older and larger teammates I could not count on being the fastest sprinter on this team. Somewhere I had read an article about running hurdles where it was explained that many beginning hurdlers make the mistake of *jumping* over a hurdle rather than *striding* over it. When you jump, the article had explained, you slow down. The proper technique was just to take an exaggerated stride over the hurdle, and exaggerate it only as much as necessary. Spend as little time in the air as possible, was the message.

This, I determined, was something I could learn to do. I would learn to run just as close to the hurdle as I could, skim over it with as little room to spare as possible, and land and be running again as soon as I could manage.

I practiced my hurdle-striding technique with fervor. I would set a match box on top of the hurdle and then brush it off with my bottom on the way over. I ended up with scrapes on my tender parts and bruises on my right knee, but I became the top hurdler on the team. Unfortunately, our coach, Mr. Parquette, had little if any experience with the sport and was probably coaching out of a manual. There was little he could do to help me, but I seemed to manage quite well on my own.

When our first track meet arrived, I was both anxious to test my skill against outside competition and terrified. The start of any race or of any game, for that matter, was an incredibly nervous experience for me. Waiting to return a kick on the football field, preparing to face off in hockey, or waiting in my blocks for the starting gun was total agony of nerves.

This first meet was a dual meet with a school called Trinity-Pawling which, we believed, had a postgraduate program for outstanding high school athletes who were not academically ready for the colleges that had recruited them. Whether this was true or not I don't know, but what was true was that Trinity-Pawling always had one or two players on their teams who could put our best athletes to shame. This spring they had a young man named Bowman, who was entered in three or four track and field events and won each of them before we came to my 120-yard low hurdles. This was scheduled as the next-to-last event of the meet, just before the four-by-one-hundred relay that traditionally climaxed a meet.

I did not cherish the idea of running the first race of my track career against this speedster. On the other hand, he had run several races already, while I was fresh. Still, I was shaking and sweating as though I were waiting to be hanged.

As we hit our first hurdle, my training seemed to have left me. I cleared the obstruction by much too big a margin and immediately found myself a stride behind. I determined not to repeat that mistake and sprinted on. My nervous energy was now magically flowing smoothly into my legs. By the time we reached the last hurdle I had almost caught up. Skimming this hurdle with probably an inch to spare, I found my landing foot hitting the cinder track just a split second earlier than his. My training had paid off, and I had the better technique. We reached the finish line at the same time and immediately threw our sweaty arms around each other.

At a small ceremony before we boarded our bus back to Millbrook, Bowman and I each received a gold medal. I also received a silver medal for running the first leg of the relay, which we had lost, as did my three teammates. On the bus back to school, I remember pressing the two medals against my chest and crying.

I ran that same event at every meet for two years and was never defeated. Once my mother actually came to Millbrook just to see me run. Uncle Arthur's son George drove her up from New Canaan where she was visiting, and they stood on the grassy bank above the cinder track. After my race, when it had been announced over the public address system that I had broken my own school record by a fraction of a second, I went up to Mother hoping for some words of praise. "You know, Yulian," Mother said in Polish, "I watched you from the side while you were running. You could be so much better looking if we fixed your nose. I will give you *three* thousand dollars to let me get it fixed." Buoyed by my recent triumph, I laughed at Mother as cousin George smiled.

Feeling herself outnumbered, Mother said, "I'm cold. I want to go back."

In the final event of the last meet of my senior year, having already won the hurdles, I was running the first leg of the relay. After the first fifty yards, I found myself even with the other runner and straining to pull away from him. I remembered hearing our coach tell one of our other sprinters, on more than one occasion, to lift his knees high as he ran. Perhaps this was something I should apply now. I concentrated on lifting my knees as I ran and, lo and behold, found myself pulling away from the other boy. I passed the baton a stride or two ahead of the other team and we went on to win the race. But I had also learned a technique to improve my running speed. Ironically, I never got to run competitively again.

I graduated from Millbrook in June of 1950, and I had been accepted by Colgate University for the coming fall. But this was to be a special summer for me. I had proclaimed my future profession to be journalism, and Mother had used her friendship with Edwin James, managing editor of the *New York Times*, to secure a summer job for me as copyboy. I would commute to this job from the Szyks' house in New Canaan, and I suggested to my former Rumsey roommate, Rod Hodgins—whose parents had just moved to Sarasota, Florida, following the success of *Mr. Blandings Builds His Dream House*—that he join me.

The Szyks had a guest house at the back of their ten-acre estate. This guest house was one room, the size of a small bedroom, with no bath, kitchen, or running water. It did have electricity and a front porch and was surrounded by wildly growing vegetation over five feet high.

And I had acquired a car. Two hundred dollars had bought me a ten-year-old Dodge with a serious reluctance to climb hills once properly warmed up. It appears that warm oil would seep into the clutch, making it slip and forcing one to approach hills like a pole-vaulter. Cars of that vintage were not built to last as long as they are today, and a ten-year-old car was considered a jalopy rather than a trusted elder vehicle.

But there were no hills between the Szyks and the train station—except for the driveway, and I soon learned to build up enough speed before making the right angle turn into the driveway to usually make it to the top. With a few housekeeping purchases, such as a used refrigerator, and furniture borrowed from the main house, Rod and I became commuters. A phone call from his dad had secured for him the post of office boy at Time Incorporated, the home of *Time*, *Life*, and *Fortune*.

I should have taken it as an omen when on the first day of my journalism career, the *New York Times* got its slogan wrong. Where it had always carried the boast "All the News That's Fit to Print" in two banks at the upper left-hand corner of page one, this edition proclaimed, "That's Fit to Print All the News."

The newsroom where I worked was a vast space full of desks, typewriters, and telephones and a residual smell of cigarettes. The desks were mostly unoccupied during the hours that I worked, since the vast majority of activity took place in the evening. Near the station where we copyboys sat stood a horseshoe-shaped table which, in the evening, would be occupied by the news editors, each with a pot of paste, a brush, and a pair of long scissors in front of him.

As the newest occupant of the lowest rung on the journalistic ladder, I was given the title of "Paste pot Editor." My first job every morning was to remove the crust from the top of the paste pots and fill them with fresh paste. Then we would sit—reading, doodling, or playing cards—till somebody yelled, "Copy!" Then you would be sent on an errand that could range from bringing a cup of coffee from the cafeteria upstairs, to going to buy a copy of a reportedly subversive magazine without saying who sent you, to helping the publisher's wife find a taxi.

Several times I stayed behind for a while to watch the night shift in operation. Many of the desks in the back of the room were occupied by busily typing or telephoning reporters, filling the room with cigarette smoke and occasionally yelling, "Copy!" Then they would hand a story to a night shift copyboy to deliver to an editor at breakneck speed. At the horseshoe-shaped editor's table, shirt-sleeved, middle-aged men sat blue-penciling, cutting, pasting, and sending copy to the composing room via a pneumatic tube system.

Several of the other copyboys, the ones who were using this as a first rung in their journalistic careers, I found out, had master's degrees in journalism. But this was usually kept secret from the men around the editors' table. None of them, it was believed, held such a degree, and many had been heard to express disdain for "book-learned journalists."

Even I understood this dynamic. They were afraid that these book-learned copyboys might know or think they knew things that they, older men, didn't. They didn't even use the word *journalism*. They were *newspaper men*. They had learned their trade in the streets and the press rooms, and that, they professed, was the proper way to do it.

I took this one step further. When I graduated from Colgate in four years with my English degree and no book-learned journalism in sight, I decided I would stand in higher favor with the newspaper establishment. If there were holes in this logic, my natural prejudice against schooling concealed them nicely.

Now that I had my own car and a salary, my evenings with Susan became more frequent, and we paired one of her girlfriends, I think her name was Betty, with Rod. A year ahead of me in school, Susan had just finished her freshman year at Jackson College, the women's arm of Tufts College (now Tufts University) in Medford, Massachusetts, outside of Boston. She was already excelling at field hockey and basketball.

Her eleven o'clock curfew remained, making dates still awkward. We would often drop Rod and Betty off at a movie and then just drive around with Susan asleep, her head on my shoulder, until curfew time. This was not great fun for me, and I marveled at Susan's ability to drop off to sleep so quickly at so early an hour. But I knew the stress that her war-damaged father created at home and was glad to be providing a kind of haven.

Chapter Thirteen

As our journalistic summer dwindled to its end, I drove Rod to Idlewild Airport (now JFK) on Long Island for his flight to Sarasota to spend some time with his parents before going off to Harvard. I recall that this was the day when we changed back from daylight saving time and I miscalculated, giving us two hours to kill before boarding time.

On the drive home I contemplated my own coming experience at Colgate. The past four years had taught me that my nature wasn't as totally bad as I had believed it to be during my Rumsey days. Above all, Susan, a popular New Canaan girl, found me acceptable—or at least sufficiently acceptable to date me. In addition, I had just completed a summer holding down an actual job. I had reported for work on time every morning, satisfied my supervisors, and managed to get home every evening. My Millbrook career had been a mixed bag of successes and failures, not quite the bleak image of uninterrupted personal disaster that I had imagined for myself while at Rumsey.

My problem, I suddenly realized, was that I thought of myself as a failure. My mother thought of herself as an achiever, and she was. If, like her, I was to think of myself an achiever, then I would achieve. And if I thought of myself as a leader, as one of the boys who told others what to do and to whom they listened, the kind of boy I had always envied, then, maybe, I would become one as well.

In schools I had attended prior to Millbrook, the role had been prohibited to me simply by the fact of language. In the French school I had attended in Warsaw I had known no French and in the Brazilian school I had known only a few words of Portuguese. I had looked at the boys or girls who set the rules for our activities with a guilty jealousy. So now that I was about to begin a new life at Colgate, among new people, I determined that I would think of myself not only as a success, but also as a leader among my peers. If I was able to convince myself of this, I would, *maybe*, make it all come to pass.

As a symbol of the new person I had become, I also decided to change my nickname of Paddy, a great improvement over the despised Julian, to what I considered the even less vulnerable Pat.

Getting to Colgate for the start of orientation week was a problem. There was no train service to the farm village of Hamilton, in the very center of New York State, where Colgate's beautiful hilly campus was situated. The five-hour drive from the New York area is beautiful, but freshmen and sophomores, the catalog informed me, were not allowed to bring cars to school. When I informed Mother, by telephone, of these facts, her response was, "So how do they want you to get there?"

There was an obvious answer to her question, but I soon realized that she and Pierre were not about to drive nine hours to New Canaan just to give me a lift to school. "You'd better figure something out," she told me. Then she used a French expression that translates loosely into, *Man up to the situation.*

Fortunately, we freshmen were supplied with a list of our new classmates, and I discovered a Leon Durant living in neighboring Darien. I called Leon, introduced myself as fellow freshman, Pat Padowicz, and explained that my parents' car had just blown a rod. After consulting with his parents, Leon invited me to ride with them. My theory about seeing myself a success was working. I had reached out and solved my problem. Life was going to be a great deal more pleasant from then on.

Major was no longer working for the Szyks, so Jimmy the gardener drove me to the Durants' house. I had one suitcase, and my aunt had slipped me a twenty dollar bill.

Colgate University stood on a hill overlooking the village of Hamilton. Farming is the local industry. In 1819 when six Baptist ministers and seven laymen obtained a charter to open a university, prospective students had to be assured that the local Indians were friendly. Among college's first trustees was one William Colgate, founder of a soap company. In Colgate lore, the story has become thirteen ministers saying thirteen prayers before pooling thirteen dollars to start what they first called Madison College.

When the Durants and I arrived they treated me to lunch at the Colgate Inn in the village. Before saying goodbye, Mr. Durant asked if I had everything I needed, including sheets, blankets, and cash. I assured him that I did.

I also had some additional things. One was the knowledge that the ocean of freshmen around me was made up of individuals, just as anxious about their new surroundings as I was and some even away from home for the first time. I, on the other hand, was well experienced in homesickness, general confusion, and things not being what one expected. The second was my new, invulnerable name. And the third was the hypothesis, and I knew it to be just a hypothesis,

that if I persevered with my self-image of success and leadership, these qualities would come to me.

I actually laughed when I discovered that members of
the administration had studied the photographs and preferred forms of address we had sent in with our acceptance
forms, and I was now greeted as Paddy by friendly looking
adult strangers. The plan for my new nickname had gone
slightly awry, but the fact that I was able to laugh at it
was in perfect harmony with my hypothesis.

I shared a small bedroom with a boy whose name I
don't remember and a living room with two more, whose
names have escaped me as well. Mindful of my resolve to
think of myself as both an academic success and a leader
among my peers, I forced myself to speak above my normal volume, to stifle my stammer, and to adopt a certain
swagger in my bearing. Having recently seen a musical
film in which college football players were much admired
by their fellow students, I reported for freshman football.
I had vacillated over whether to do this or not. I had no
great desire to crash my body against others, but if I was
to be true to my commitment, I had no choice but to suck
up my concerns and offer my body to the glory of Colgate
and my own ego.

During freshman week the coach of the freshman team
had told us all that no one got cut from the team. People
who quit the team were people who *decided* to quit. This
was encouraging. That I had not gotten any playing time
on the Millbrook varsity was not because I had been found
wanting. Mr. Kneutson had never given me a chance to
show what I could do. Maybe the Colgate coach would
discover that, armed with my new winner attitude, I could
do a great deal.

I was by far the smallest student showing up for practice,
but as we stood around listening to the coach talk, I told

myself over and over that I could take care of myself. Yeah, I might be small, but I was tough. And I was damned fast.

On the first day, there was no contact, and I took hand-offs from the quarterback with the best of the prospective running backs. Then on the second day, the coach placed us in circles of five, with a sixth in the middle. The idea was that one of the five would call the name of the one in the middle and charge him. The one in the middle was supposed to turn to face and counter the charge with his own shoulder.

I was the first in my group to be in the middle. Some-one would call my name, and I would turn to face him in time to be knocked to the ground by a force I had never encountered before, as two hundred plus pounds crashed into my one hundred and twenty pound frame. I accepted four of these bone-rattling crashes and realized that the body I had inherited from my petite mother wasn't cut out for college-level football. My successes would have to be achieved in the classroom. I walked off the field, handed my pads to the team manager, showered, walked up the hill to my dorm, and never put on pads again.

What I did do, however, was loyally attend the fresh-man team's home games. A leader, I reasoned, when he was unable actually to lead his soldiers in battle due to circumstances beyond his control, would express his sup-port in any way he could. In my case it would be shouting encouragement from the stands. One cold, rainy afternoon, as my fellow freshmen battled some other school's fresh-men, I was the only spectator.

How my class as a whole viewed my leadership, I had no way of knowing. Two of my suite mates, however, found it amusing. Best friends from somewhere in New Jersey, they tended to adopt a condescending attitude toward things in general, took to calling me "Sarge," and to making fun of the letters I daily wrote to Susan. Taking charge of my own problem, I asked to be transferred to another room.

My new roommate was a young man named Erazim "Raza" Kohak, who had spent the war under Nazi occupation in his native Czechoslovakia. He had been in the United States for only three years, but his English was as good as mine except for his accent. Having arrived in America at the age of nine, I had apparently slipped in just under the deadline because people tell me I have no foreign accent at all. Raza had not been so lucky. But with him speaking Czech and me Polish, two very similar languages, we could communicate in private to the consternation of our classmates.

The first week of classes presented a problem. You had to buy textbooks at the bookstore, and I, with the fifteen dollars I had left after an evening of drinking beer at the Colgate Inn with my classmates—something my leadership role had obliged me to do—did not have enough to buy even one book. I am sure that the catalog must have mentioned something about buying books, but reading instructions is not something I've ever been good at.

When I called Mother for more money, I could hear her tell Pierre, "I'm sure he spent all his money on beer." Experience had taught me not to point out that she had given me no money. When I explained that I could do little learning without textbooks, Mother promised to send me some, but warned me that I couldn't do this any more. Ten days later, a check for another twenty arrived.

But, of course, attending class without having read the assignment was nothing new to me. Motivated by my new attitude toward life, I listened attentively in class, spoke up when I had something to say, and by the middle of the fall

anto anto? anto

semester discovered myself on the way to making the honor roll. Nothing like that had ever happened to me before.

Then my parents came to see what Colgate was all about. Colgate has a lovely campus, and they were both charmed. Having heard that I was taking a course in the Russian language, Mother asked to meet my Russian professor.

I had signed up for the course in an effort to get an easy credit among the freshman courses designed to determine who was proper college material and who was not. Russian is quite similar to my native Polish, though it uses a different alphabet. Everyone in Poland knew a few Russian phrases, the way Americans know some Spanish ones. I had told Dr. Parry, a bald bullfrog of a man with a deep Russian accent, that I spoke Polish and he had given me appropriately tougher assignments. But Mother speaking with my teacher was something from which no good could come, and I demurred.

I explained to Mother that this would not be a good idea, but she turned to Pierre and said, "He's jealous because his professor will find out that I speak better Russian than Julian does."

I tried to explain that that was not the case, but Mother just laughed, lit a cigarette, and motioned Pierre to drive on. As we pulled up in front of the little granite building that housed Colgate's one-man Russian department, I made a final plea from the backseat. But Mother just set her jaw, fixed her silk scarf in Pierre's rearview mirror, and went into the building. Pierre chain-smoked while we waited without ever looking at me.

Some forty-five minutes later, a beaming Dr. Parry led my smiling mother out to the car, chatting, of course, in Russian. As he held the door open for Mother, Dr. Parry wagged a finger at me.

"He will give you As from now on, you'll see," Mother said as we drove down the hill to lunch at the Colgate Inn. Over lunch, Mother explained how she had told Dr. Parry that her mother was Russian and we all always spoke Russian at home. When Pierre and I both suggested that that might increase the professor's expectation of me, Mother pooh-poohed our fears. The next marking period saw my Russian grade drop from its B+ to a D, dashing my hope of making the honor roll.

Social life at Colgate, I learned, was centered in the fraternities. Being an all-male college, Colgate boasted thirteen Greek letter fraternities with national affiliations, housed in fine stone or brick residences across the street from the campus. Most active in the South, the majority of these fraternities had membership restricted to Caucasian Christians. While some took in "local" brothers whose names and photographs would never appear on the national rolls, for young men of social conscience there was something sticky about Greek letter membership. A fourteenth, independent, and strictly liberal fraternity, the Colgate Commons Club, existed on campus, occupying half of one of the dormitories and using the Old Stone Jug, a downtown bar with a small restaurant attached, as its official eating facility.

Except for the large dining hall on the second floor of the student union and the bookstore/coffee shop in the basement of one of the dorms, the university offered no facilities for socializing other than the fraternities. The little town of Hamilton had a small movie theater, the Colgate Inn with its pub, a weekly newspaper, and an assortment of stores, businesses, and bars. The nearest women's college was Cazenovia Junior College, twenty miles away, where on Friday and Saturday night a Colgate freshman lucky enough to get a ride could walk into a dorm, speak with the student on desk duty, and find himself with a date for a couple of hours, until the dorm's curfew at eleven.

Fraternities held weekend parties to which one could invite a girl from back home or from a nearby women's school. In addition, brothers with cars could provide transportation for weekend trips. As a result, some 90 percent of Colgate sophomores, juniors, and seniors belonged to one fraternity or another. But because the rushing, or recruiting, of freshmen by fraternities was highly competitive, it was also highly regulated, and freshmen were not allowed in fraternity houses until rushing week in the second semester. Intense as the rushing was, the anticipation as to which fraternity might want you when rushing week came around was even more so. Joining a fraternity was a commitment for life. Not only did a fraternity present you with companions and a social life during your college days, but it also gave you valuable business and social contacts for after college.

There was fighting going on in Korea at the time, and young men my age were being drafted. The way to stay out of the draft was to sign up for ROTC (Reserve Officers' Training Corps). This exempted you until graduation, at which time you were commissioned a second lieutenant and had a three-year service commitment. Fond of uniforms and parades as I'd been and not eager to go to Korea, I signed up for Colgate's air force program. In addition to some classroom activities, the ROTC program also held drill in front of the student union every Friday afternoon. After drill, we were free till classes on Monday, and that's when I discovered the now-lost art of hitchhiking.

The ROTC uniform was a help in this, since people tended to take you for a GI on leave from Korea, and we freshmen would soon be out alongside the highways with our thumbs out. While sophomores were not allowed to have cars either, most were pledges in fraternities where they had a social life. For us freshmen, the only social life available locally was in the pub room at the Colgate Inn.

It was three hundred miles to Medford, where Susan was attending Jackson College. With luck, I could ring the doorbell at her dorm before the evening curfew. Susan would usually have made arrangements for me to sleep in an empty bed in one of the men's dorms, and Saturday morning we would walk down to a car rental garage and rent a car for two days. The purpose of the car was not so much for transportation as to park in some secluded spot and "neck."

With Susan as my instructor, I had learned that at this stage of a relationship, in other words *going steady*, engaging tongues was permissible, as was an occasional brush of the hand across a fully clothed breast. From my dorm mates back at Millbrook, I had learned that techniques existed for accessing a bare nipple with the hand and even that nectar where the thighs meet, but the techniques themselves had never been revealed to me. As we sat in our parked rented car, our arms around one another and our legs intertwined at the knees, my fingers would explore possible entryways into Susan's clothing, only to be pushed away by an elbow accompanied by, "Don't do that." By seven PM on Sunday, with the car returned, I and a lot of other college men would be on the road back to our own schools. I was never late for Monday morning classes, but I never learned much on those Mondays.

Sometimes I would invite company for these long trips. Susan would arrange a date for my companion, and he and I would share the cost of the car rental as well as provide each other with company on the long treks there and back. Strangely enough, while the dates that Susan provided were always good-looking and seemed friendly enough, I was never able to get any classmate to make the trip more than once.

Each trip, from one point to the other, would usually be covered by an average of six rides. Often our ride would be from a couple with a son in Korea, and we would answer questions in very vague terms, trying to conceal the fact that we were not really in the service. One time, late into the night on our trip back to school, my companion, Mike, and I got picked up by two women probably three or four years older than ourselves. "Oh, I'm so tired of driving," the driver said and asked Mike to take over. Her companion immediately got into the backseat with me.

She removed her jacket and her shoes, placed her hands behind her head, and closed her eyes. There was the unmistakable scent of deodorant at work, and I had a strong suspicion that something was expected of me at this point, but no idea of what that might be. Several scenarios passed through my mind, each with two possible endings, one of which always had Mike and me back by the side of the road with our thumbs out and my face red and sore. On the other hand, the alternate ending, in its multiple versions, was quite delightful. While none of the scenarios played out that night, I did enjoy replaying them in my mind for some weeks to come.

And each completed round-trip, however cold, lonely, or frustrating it may have been, placed another layer of soundproof insulation between me and the inconsolable little Julian, whimpering on his Rumsey bed.

Colgate, I learned, had a sacred tradition, namely its rivalry with nearby Syracuse University. Each fall Colgate played Syracuse in football, and over the years of the rivalry little Colgate, we were told, had beaten big Syracuse most of the time. In the thirties, in fact, under the coaching of one Andy Kerr, Colgate had dominated collegiate football. In 1932, the year I was born, the team had not had one point scored against it throughout the entire season. Expected to go to the Rose Bowl on New Year's Day, no team could be found to oppose them, earning the label "undefeated, untied, un-scored upon, and uninvited."

The ensuing two decades, however, had not been kind to Colgate football. Football programs in other, much larger colleges and universities had grown while the idea of spending one's college football career playing in the little village of Hamilton before grandstands filled with local farmers was not very attractive to the nation's top athletes. In addition, Colgate maintained strict academic standards. As a result, against the much larger Syracuse University, which could attract such players as Jim Brown, Floyd Little, Larry Csonka, and Donovan McNabb, Colgate stood little chance.

But this reality did not seem to have reached the staff and students in charge of maintaining school spirit. When the two teams met on the gridiron in Syracuse, we freshmen had been told, the Colgate section of the stadium always outshouted the far larger crowd on the opposing side. The fact that "Colgate" was far easier to shout than "Syracuse" was not considered a factor.

The week before the Syracuse game it was traditional to invade one another's campus and perpetrate symbolic and creative pranks such as painting a stripe of your school's color (maroon for Colgate, orange for Syracuse) down the center of the main thoroughfare, stealing the clapper out of the chapel bell (to be ceremoniously returned after the game), and kidnapping the team mascot. Conversely, the penalty for getting caught on the other school's campus was having one's head shaved and being held hostage till after the game.

On our campus, self-appointed patrols roamed the area, stopping cars without Colgate parking stickers and generally imitating Soviet secret police. I volunteered my services to a group barricading one entrance to the campus for a portion of several nights. I can't say that we captured anyone.

I had suggested to my parents that they drive down from Montreal for the Syracuse game and the ensuing parties, which they might enjoy, but Mother's response was, "Don't be silly." On the other hand, during the spring semester, they did make another four- or five-hour drive to visit me.

Before reaching Hamilton, they found a house in the town of Madison, a few minutes away, where the landlady had a comfortable room to rent to weekend visitors. "She has a shed where you can hide your car," Mother said over lunch at the Colgate Inn. "I have already talked to her about it. Why don't you hitchhike down to New Canaan, bring your car up, and keep it in the woman's shed."

"We're not supposed to have cars anywhere where we can have access to them from school," I answered.

"How will they ever know?" Mother said. "Just don't be foolish and drive it on campus." Then she added, "That way Pierre and I won't have to drive you to and from school anymore." Not that they ever *had* driven me to or from school.

"When *I* was in school," Pierre added in French, "we—" and he made a spitting sound and an accompanying Gallic gesture, "—at the rules."

In the end I accepted Mother's logic and Pierre's challenge to my manhood, and the following weekend I was hitching my way to New Canaan, through the Catskill Mountains, to fetch my 1940 Dodge. I got picked up by a young Catholic priest. He had just been assigned to a parish somewhere in the Catskills, and he wasn't happy about it. He called the area "Kikeskills" and proceeded to express his contempt for "Kikes" till he pulled up in front of his new rectory and invited me in for something to eat. Fearing that I might become that something to eat, I declined.

Returning to Colgate under my own power was a heady feeling. My route to the rented garage in Madison took me directly past the campus, and I drove with one hand over the lower part of my face. Then I became very popular with certain fellow freshmen with whom I shared my secret.

Cautious by nature, I did not risk driving near campus again. But my biweekly trips to Medford and Susan became much more pleasant, though not without their own set of difficulties. Leaving Medford around eight in the evening, I would usually find my way impeded by a fog that my headlights could not penetrate beyond a couple of feet. I would try to place myself behind a truck, whose tail lights I could clearly see, and hope that he was heading the same way I was.

I discovered that driving all night was not as easy as partying all night. My eyes would become fatigued and each passing pair of headlights a hazard. On more than one occasion I found myself dozing.

On the other hand, it was easier now to find company for these trips. We would take turns driving and sleeping. On one such trip, after driving the first few hours I turned the wheel over to my companion and stretched out in the backseat. I was soon surprised to find the car inclined to the right at an alarmingly steep angle and sat up to see what the trouble was. My companion assured me that he was "getting the hang of it." It turned out that he had never driven a car before.

Like any college, Colgate had a newspaper, the *Colgate Maroon*. Freshmen were invited to *scrub* a position on the *Maroon*. Scrubbing was what you did to join any activity, and it meant tryouts and, I supposed, rejections. As a veteran of the *New York Times*, I felt scrubbing for such a job to be beneath me. Besides, there was the risk of another rejection.

On the other hand, the town of Hamilton boasted a weekly newspaper, the *Mid-York Weekly,* a real newspaper staffed not by college students playing newspaperman but by professionals. My *New York Times* credentials might get me a part-time job here that would look good on my future resume, provide me with some pocket money, and one-up my classmates who were scrubbing our make-believe school paper.

To my great surprise, the managing editor of the *Mid-York Weekly* hired me. I was put to work rewriting news stories submitted by stringers, local housewives who reported on the Grange meetings, birthday celebrations, and betrothals within their community. It wasn't till later that I would realize that I had outsmarted myself. While I was putting reports of calf births and retirement ceremonies into appropriate journalistic prose, my counterparts on the *Colgate Maroon* were learning to write editorials on university policy as well as national affairs, to interview visiting celebrities, and to make-up a newspaper page. My hypothesis about thinking myself a winner wasn't foolproof.

Chapter Fourteen

Soon after the start of the second semester was fraternity rushing season at Colgate. Starting on a certain date, teams of fraternity brothers would go out to visit certain freshmen in their dorms for strictly limited periods of time after dinner, to determine which ones they would like to know better as potential new members or pledges to their house. These visits would be followed by invitations in our mailboxes from this house or that for a lunch, a dinner, or a tunk. *Tunk* was strictly a Colgate term for an all-male cocktail party.

These affairs would go on for about a week, with nightly meetings in each house to determine which freshmen had made a positive enough impression to be invited to pledge or at least to come for a second look. Much like the drafting of college players by professional athletic teams, actually pledging a freshman was not permitted until a certain hour of a certain day, after the lunches and the dinners and the tunks were all over with.

Among us freshmen, the anticipation as to which fraternities would send delegations to visit you in your room and what invitations would be in your mailbox as a result was unbearable. To some, lifetime careers were at stake, to say nothing of one's standing on campus. Lurking in the lowest layers of my own consciousness was the question of whether it was Pat or Julian that the fraternity members were really seeing.

The visits to our dorm rooms didn't tell us too much. With most freshmen living in four-man suites and the brothers on their most polite insurance-salesman behavior, it was difficult to tell which of the four roommates they were actually looking over. They would show up outside our door in groups of four, showered and shaved and waiting for the visiting time to begin. Then they would knock politely the moment the clock struck the designated hour.

After introductions all around, the visitors would usually comment on the room, the poster you might have on your wall of Ted Williams, racing cars, Rita Hayworth, or that new girl, Marilyn Monroe. This might lead to a half hour of walking on eggshells (I think the period was half an hour) at the end of which all would say good-bye and four brothers from another fraternity would come in. At the end of the visiting period the brothers would hold meetings in their houses to evaluate the freshmen they had visited and we freshmen would speculate which of the roommates they had actually been interested in and who might get an invitation where.

On the first day of invitations, I received just one lunch invitation. Well, I thought, that was because earlier in the semester when formal tours of the fraternity houses were being conducted, I had decided not to participate. On the other hand, it could also have been because everyone but me could see that the self-assured Pat was just a big act.

The invitation was from the one independent fraternity on campus, the one that didn't have a house at the bottom of the hill but occupied the west section of West Hall dormitory on the hill and had a meeting room on the ground floor, the Colgate Commons Club.

Of course this represented only one lunch out of many. For all I knew there might be invitations from any number of fraternities in tomorrow's mail. On the other hand, I had a strong suspicion that I was deluding myself, and if the Commons Club, where I knew no one, were interested in my unworthy self I should make the best of it.

The lunch, held in a private dining room of the student union building, was very pleasant and afterward I was invited to attend that evening's dinner as well. I responded that I hadn't received the prescribed invitation but was told not to worry about such a technicality. I didn't and showed up for dinner.

Of the several other freshmen at this meal, I don't think I knew any. Bob Geiser, a brother who had sat beside me at lunch and issued the dinner invitation, was sitting beside me again. I don't remember what we talked about but we did make cordial conversation through the whole meal, a feat I had not considered myself capable of. Then Bob asked me to come to that evening's tunk as well. Suddenly I had the heady feeling that these people were interested in me. But I had had feelings like that before only to be bitterly disappointed, and I now told myself to hold my enthusiasm in check.

The tunk was held in the Commons Club's meeting room in West Hall, and I was pleased to see my roommate, Raza, there among others. As I sipped my free beer from a waxed paper cup, Bob asked me if I had any questions about the Commons Club, to which I said that I didn't, though I assured him that I held great respect for boys who refused to join one of the shamefully discriminating Greek letters. In truth, I hadn't even known the Commons Club to be a fraternity; I'd thought it some sort of common interest organization. Bob asked how I liked what I had seen of the Commons Club so far, and I said that I was very impressed. Then Bob Geiser and a Bob Reith invited me to come upstairs to their room. I followed nervously, because I was quite sure now that I was going to be asked to pledge and to do it in violation of university rules.

Sure enough, whispering though we were now behind closed doors, one of the Bobs asked me how I would feel about becoming a member. Without a house, without dining facilities, without those Greek letters you could paste in the rear window of your car, and without a secret handshake, I didn't see much glamour to membership. On the other hand, I had never been asked to join anything before.

But what if, at this very moment, my mailbox at the student union at the bottom of the hill contained one or even several invitations from Greek letter fraternities? By saying yes to this invitation now, I would be blowing my chances of ever joining one. I would say yes now and sign, and in the morning I would find invitations from three different fraternities. How would I feel then?

I could certainly say that I needed time to think it over and check my mailbox first. But the offer might not be made again. I might get no other offers from anyone, and then where would I be? I would spend my next three and a half years at Colgate as one of the few that didn't get asked to join *any* fraternity. They were called *independents* and, of course, they all claimed that they weren't interested in fraternity life. But everyone knew that the disinterest was mutual. I would be one of them, standing on the stairs to the student union dining hall every evening along with the freshmen, and everyone would know.

But these two Bobs and the fraternity they represented were risking punishment for signing me up illegally. There must have been a meeting this evening, just before the tunk, when they had discussed me and decided, by vote, that they wanted me in their fraternity, as one of them.

God, how I would like to have been a fly on the wall at that meeting.

Of course, if they had decided so quickly that they wanted me as a member, me whom no other fraternity even wanted to cast an eye over, what sort of group could they be? I mean, how with it, how hip could they be? But Bob and Bob were both such nice guys. They had extended an invitation to me so how could I turn them down?

All right, I knew how important a decision this was. Fraternity membership lasted your whole life. Fraternity brothers you could call on for help at any time, in terms of business and career. Greek letter fraternities had thousands of members throughout the country, many highly influential. A secret handshake and you had a new ally in whatever you were doing. How many Colgate Commons Club members were out there in the world?

But how could I say no to Bob and Bob?

"I would be honored to," I said and took the book. On the left-hand page I could see that there was a list of names showing through from the other side. The right-hand page was completely blank. One of the Bobs pointed to the first line of the blank page. I would be the first to sign. I signed.

Lightning didn't strike. Instead, one of the Bobs spoke words that I will remember for the rest of my pre-addled life. "That's great," he said. "Now we can build our pledge class around you." Sweeter words had never been laid on my ego before, and few times since.

As the three of us went back downstairs, I walked with a light step. I looked around at the other freshmen attending the tunk and savored the knowledge that I was now not only a member of a group but one whose name would be used to attract other prospective members. I saw Bob Geiser give a covert nod to one of two brothers talking with my roommate. The three of them headed toward the stairs. I knew where they were going. They had probably told Raza that I had already signed, hoping that that would help him to decide. I had the definite sense that I was a foot taller than everyone else in the room.

For the rest of rushing week, I ate my lunches and suppers in that little dining room on the ground floor of the student union. I attended the tunks, and brothers treated me like an old friend. I had never been treated quite that way before. I got introduced to other freshmen who had signed the book secretly. For the first time in my life I spoke easily and confidently at a social function.

When college life returned to normal after the rushing disruption, it was a whole new normal for me. Making my cautious way down the slippery, snow-covered hill to meals, I would hear the name Pat mentioned and turn to find a fellow Commons Club pledge or even a brother, slipping and sliding his way beside me. Coming out of the cafeteria line with my tray, I would see a table with several fellow pledges waving to me to join them. This kind of thing had never happened to me before.

I could see similar groupings taking place in the dining hall as newly related pledges of other fraternities hailed each other with the enthusiasm of newly formed friendships. But their very enthusiasm seemed to mark a difference between them and us. The quiet smiles of my fellow Commons Club pledges, the wordless moving over to make room, bespoke an acceptance that made the others' enthusiasm seem artificial, like the forced smiles and the air kisses that I had always seen grownups exchange. And on the second or maybe third day of this post-rushing period I began to realize that those others were just beginning a life in which an expression of enthusiasm was the required admission to their daily events.

While I was happy to be welcomed by my new fellow pledges, neither I nor they felt it necessary to give noise to that pleasure. And then I had a further realization—somewhere in their lives, though certainly to a lesser degree than I, my fellow pledges had probably shared my experience of feeling rejected. And the joke-cracking, backslapping of the Greek letter pledges was a fear-driven defense against what was commonplace to me, what I and those in my new group had come to an acknowledgement of and an accommodation with. Of course, to suspect that my large, bumpy nose and my Polish name, which to American ears sounded Semitic, might have something to do with the lack of invitations in my mailbox was not something I considered.

In addition I had the feeling that my fellow pledges were looking to me for leadership. The leadership role which I had been searching for on my arrival and then forgotten had suddenly materialized.

I immediately made myself busy in fraternity activities. Having learned that trying to study was a waste of my time, I had more time for this than other members. I learned at a club meeting that at spring party weekend, to which I was planning to invite Susan, we pledges were expected to provide a skit for entertainment. I immediately volunteered to write and direct this skit and was just as immediately accepted. Then I went for a long walk in search of an idea.

Television was still a novelty in 1951, especially in Hamilton where the Commons Club set received just one channel clearly. My skit, I decided, would be three or four five-minute television shows of which I can only remember two. In one a foreign dignitary responds to an interviewer in unintelligible English, which seemed funny in concept. The other was the finale in which three elderly char women, I among them, come into the studio to mop the floor after programming ends for the day and discover that a camera has been left on by accident. They discuss the fact that the fourth char woman, Myrtle, is absent because she is attending a party weekend at the Colgate Commons Club and, in the event that she might be watching, proceed to give her some partying advice in a song to the tune of "Take Me out to the Ball Game." To the college mind of that day, this was funny.

Susan came by train from Boston, and I picked her up at the Utica train station. With money from my job at the *Mid-York Weekly*, I secured a room for her for those two nights in some faculty member's house. Friday night the parties were in the fraternities, and I had a leading part in decorating our meeting room with streamers and sparklers. It turned out that several of our members were musically inclined and had even formed a dance band.

The second evening there was a dance in the gymnasium. Susan was beautiful in a strapless gown, and I had some approximation of a tuxedo. After the dance, with no curfew, we looked for a discreet spot to park. By moonlight, we found an open gate leading to a cow pasture off a country road. We drove down into the pasture and proceeded to do what I believed college students did in this kind of situation. It wasn't what college students do nowadays, and I don't remember the details, but I do recall experiencing a thrill or two that I had not experienced before.

Then it was time to get some sleep, and I put the car in reverse. But it wouldn't budge. The wheels had sunk into the soft ground. I tried and tried, but we ended up with Susan sleeping in the back seat and me in front. When dawn broke, I was able to stop a passing farmer with his tractor and a chain. I explained to him that my sister and I had wandered off the road by mistake.

Early that spring the tryouts for Colgate's track team were announced. I had high hopes for this activity. It could, I knew, lead to the Olympics. I showed up in my spikes at the appointed time. The coach asked the group of us to run a certain distance at three-quarters speed. I arrived dead last and, accepting the reality that my high school speed was no match for the competition I now faced, I did not show up again. My dreams of making the Olympic team disintegrated. It was only years later that I realized that when a coach asks team prospects to run at three-quarters speed, only a fool like myself would run at anything but full speed.

Then, in the middle of that same semester, I got a call to the dean's office. It seemed that the subterfuge regarding my car had been discovered, and I received a suspension from school. I had to go home. I could be reinstated on a certain date in time for final exams, Dean Kalgrin informed me, if my parents came to Colgate on that date and petitioned him in person.

That night, as I huddled under my blanket, I could hear little Julian quite clearly as he whimpered in his bunk. I had witnessed public suspensions and expulsions at Rumsey and empathized with the pall of disgrace on that fellow student, not far short of a public hanging. While my culpability was somewhat mitigated by my parents' involvement in the conspiracy, the shame, at least of being caught, was all mine. What was worse was knowing that the Szyks were not in New Canaan at this time, and the following day I would have to head my nefarious vehicle north toward Montreal.

I found the concern over my parents' wrath somewhat overblown. Mother, it turned out, saw in this an opportunity to introduce me to the daughters of some members of Montreal's diplomatic corps, and Pierre gave me a beer and told me about his cadet days at Saumur, France's elite cavalry officers' school.

He took me to see his office and introduce me to his boss, the consul. In our travels westward through Europe escaping the advancing Nazis, I had visited many consulates as Mother negotiated for a visa to the next country, and I was disappointed by the mundane nature of this one. I don't know what I had expected, but this was a couple small offices on the second floor of a small downtown office building. There was no elevator, and Pierre had to struggle up the stairs with his artificial leg and his cane.

In addition, Mother explained to me that Pierre's pay was very small. If it wasn't for continued help from Reggie, they would have a difficult time making ends meet. I wondered what still kept Reggie in the picture.

One Sunday afternoon my parents informed me they had arranged a date for me. I had already told them that my relationship with Susan did not permit such activities but this, they said, was different. This girl was Polish. The family had recently arrived in Canada, her father a member of the Polish consular staff. She spoke no English or French and knew no one her age who spoke Polish. Besides, I was expected to pick her up in half an hour.

While I wasn't pleased with the way the situation had been handled, this, technically, was more of a social amenity between families of the Montreal Diplomatic Corps than it was a date. Besides which, I was bored. I dared not, of course, speculate as to where the date might lead. "How do I get to her house within half an hour?" I asked. "And where am I supposed to take her?"

It turned out that this had been arranged as well. My mother, Pierre, and I were all going to take her for a drive in the country.

Unsophisticated as I still was on the subject of boy/girl activities, I was quite aware that a drive in the country with my parents would not be particularly enjoyable to either my date or me. Still, the plans had been made, and that was that.

Pierre drove us to her house and I was dispatched to ring the doorbell. The young lady who answered the door was attractive, with the typical blonde and blue-eyed good looks of Polish women. Her name was Maryshka. When we returned to the car, I saw that Pierre and Mother had moved to the rear seat, vacating the front for us. With Pierre directing me which way to turn and Mother telling me how fast to go, we went for a drive in the country.

While I had maintained my Polish through conversations with Mother when she didn't want Pierre or Susan to understand, I found my seven-year-old's vocabulary vastly inadequate to my needs. Maryshka seemed to recognize my difficulty and carried most of the conversation's burden. Mother, who usually kibitzed in Polish, did it in English this time as she instructed me from the backseat about what stories I should tell, what questions I should ask, and what compliments I should offer, all of which I ignored. When the subject of Maryshka's limited English came up, Mother urged me to offer to teach her. The idea had occurred to me several miles earlier, but I would not give Mother the satisfaction. I assured my companion that she would learn quickly.

When we were back in Maryshka's driveway, the young woman turned back in her seat and proceeded to thank Mother and Pierre in quite good English. It was then that a remarkable thing happened. Pierre, of course, turned beet red, and there must have been some blush on my face as well, but Mother burst out laughing. "I guess the joke is on me, Miss," she said in Polish, holding out her hand.

I recalled an incident in the hotel in Rio de Janeiro, some years before, when Mother lost the diamond ring that was our only resource for the funds we would need to reach America. Mother's companion and I hung our heads in mourning for the loss, but Mother said the Polish equivalent of *no use crying over spilled milk* and suggested we go downstairs for a cup of tea to raise our spirits. On the way downstairs, we found the ring glittering in the sweepings of the rooftop beside the hotel, which a porter was just gathering. It must have been Mother's ability to see a glass nine-tenths full when others found it three-quarters empty that had set us to climbing that mountain separating occupied Poland from Hungary.

As Maryshka and I parted on her doorstep, she kissed me on the cheek. In that kiss I thought I felt empathy.

On the appointed day, the three of us drove back to Colgate—I, driving my illicit car since I had been told that I could bring it if I left the plates with the dean's secretary for keeping through the end of the school semester. Mother chose to ride with me, because she didn't really like how fast Pierre drove. My ten-year-old car was not capable of the speeds to which Pierre, with his diplomatic immunity, aspired.

At the border, the procedure was very simple. Once you declared your US citizenship and gave a place of birth, you were waved on. No passport or other identification was required. However Mother, a longtime American citizen by now, had a French diplomatic passport as well and insisted on presenting it to the man in charge of the border station. The man in charge was out running an errand, we were told, but the officer attending to us said that the man in question would be very disappointed if he learned that he had missed the wife of the French vice consul. Would we mind waiting in his office until he returned. Mother graciously agreed.

We waited some thirty minutes on folding chairs, met the man, and Mother told him that she had written a book entitled *Flight to Freedom* some eight years earlier, recounting her escape over the Carpathian Mountains from the Bolsheviks, on foot, leading a frightened little boy by the hand after being abandoned by her guide. The man marveled at her courage, sympathized with her suffering, and we were on our way again. We arrived in Hamilton two hours behind Pierre.

I got to hear Mother tell her story again, in Dean Kalgrin's office, with a response from the dean much similar to the one she had received at the border. Then Dean Kalgrin explained that the rule I had broken was there to keep freshmen from going wild their first year away from home, and my parents heartily endorsed the policy. While I knew this endorsement to be hypocrisy, I understood the need for the charade and dutifully bowed my head in shame. The dean asked if I understood the gravity of breaking the school's trust in me, and I said that I did and that I was sorry.

Then I heard Mother murmur something to Pierre and with a thump of his cane on the floor and considerable creaking of his prosthesis, Pierre stood up from his chair and proceeded to lecture me on the importance of obeying rules and being a man of honor. While Pierre and I normally conversed in French, this lecture was delivered in English. I did not really deserve to own a car, he said, and it was only the fact that they lived in Montreal that kept him from taking my car from me and selling it.

I felt tears well up in my eyes. Not for my misdeeds, but for Pierre's betrayal.

Chapter Fifteen

The summer following my freshman year I again spent commuting into New York. I had asked Mother to negotiate the *Times* job for another summer but for some reason she arranged, instead, with her friend Spyros Skouras, president of Twentieth Century-Fox Film Corporation, for me to have a job at the Roxy Theater.

When it was built in 1927 just off Times Square, the Roxy was the largest and grandest movie house in the world. Seating 5,920 people in its baroque splendor, the Roxy, named after its builder, treated its patrons to both a motion picture and a stage show on the same program. The precision of its chorus line, the Rockettes, was world renowned. The equally precise drill of the militaristically uniformed ushers as they lined up for inspection in the rotunda, then marched to their assigned posts in the orchestra, the loge, or one of the balconies, was a sight worth the price of admission.

A few years later, its builder, Sam Rothafel, built an even larger theater one block away in the Rockefeller Center complex, this time in the prevailing Art Deco style. He named it Radio City Music Hall and took the lovely Rockettes with him.

Now, in 1951, the Roxy was suffering from what the entire motion picture industry was suffering from, namely television. Its empty seats were a soundless cry of despair as operating costs made a mockery of its income. Only Radio City, still a major tourist attraction, managed to fill its seats on a regular basis.

The Roxy's owners, Twentieth Century-Fox, had appointed a Mr. Katz as manager with instructions to stop the hemorrhaging while maintaining the standards for which the Roxy was famous. This economic balancing act Mr. Katz explained to me when I reported to his office.

My title would be student assistant manager, placing me between the several assistant managers and the ushers. Like the assistant managers, I would wear a blue suit in the morning and change into a tuxedo in the afternoon. I would inspect the ushers in the rotunda when they came on duty and assign them to their various posts. Then I would be assigned a section of the theater to patrol and supervise.

All Roxy front-of-the-house employees addressed one another as Mister or Miss, the Miss being a concession to modernity and Rosie the Riveter, since the ranks of the usher corps had previously been closed to female ushers. The war had also seen the end of the military-style uniforms and drill since it was found to be more reminiscent of German troops than of our own.

The assistant managers' dressing room, behind a brocade curtained door halfway up the loge and balcony stairs, was the one place where we assistant managers could relate on a first name basis. And this was the first time that I had ever been on a first name basis with adults other than family or servants. The other four or five assistant managers were men in their thirties and forties ("modernity" hadn't added women assistant managers to our ranks), and I was the only student assistant manager until another one joined our ranks halfway through the summer. Arriving at work at various times, since our shifts were staggered throughout a twelve-hour day, we would change into our blue suits with a cup of coffee and amiable adult conversation. Lunch break, changing into tuxedos, and then dressing for the trip home provided more contact opportunities through the day.

I had never been privy to informal adult male conversation, and listening to my fellow assistant managers discuss wives, children, mortgages, baseball, plumbers, train schedules, lawnmowers, schools, in-laws, the cost of cigarettes, girlfriends, and opportunities missed was a whole new life experience. I listened eagerly to these grown men discussing subjects I had never heard discussed before. At the Szyks the talk was always world affairs and, at my parents, usually affairs of a different kind. I even had to have the term *mortgage* explained to me. But the fact that a Colgate wide receiver (we called them *ends* in those days) had been the leading pass receiver in the country during the previous season gave me the opportunity to contribute to the conversation one afternoon.

The ushers and usherettes had a lunch room where they also gathered on their breaks for conversation and cigarettes, and I spent some time there as well. Whether I was there in some managerial capacity or whether I was even supposed to be there at all I don't remember, but there I had exposure to working people of my own age. Except most recently at the Colgate Commons Club, I had never felt like a social equal among my peers, a perception of inferiority which, of course, was always quickly sensed by the others and turned into reality. But here, where my position commanded a certain level of respect, my innate desire for friendship soon made me feel accepted and even liked. While the young men and women still addressed me as Mr. Padowicz—a name many found virtually unpronounceable—and I did not sit at their long lunch table out of concern for my tuxedo, I again felt accepted by a group that I had never felt accepted by before.

After work, when my assistant manager colleagues went home to families, I would often join a group of ushers and usherettes for beer at a nearby bar. There were, among these young people, girls whom I found attractive and who seemed to be receptive to my attempts at conversation. One young lady, Madeleine, an aspiring actress with blonde hair and blue eyes, I found particularly attractive. Were I to pursue some of these opportunities for friendship further, I believed I would be able to convert one or more of them to something more intimate. But my emotions were committed to Susan, who was working as a lifeguard at a Kiwanis camp in New Canaan for the summer, and I wouldn't permit myself to do so.

Then I came upon the most memorable of my summer experiences. On Sundays the theater opened somewhat later than it did on weekdays, so the evening before when the ushers came off their shifts some of them would go bowling at the all-night bowling alley across the street until the last shift had been released. At that point they, and now I with them, piled into cars and drove out to the beach at Far Rockaway, in Queens.

It was past midnight when we arrived at the deserted beach. A half moon reflected in the still water. I saw people break away from the group and begin changing into their bathing suits in the dark. Not having had prior knowledge of this happening, I had not brought one with me.

Then I felt a hand brush my arm and heard the voice of Madeleine, one of the aspiring actresses call, "Come on, Mr. Padowicz!" As I looked up I saw three girls running toward the water holding hands. And, as I looked more carefully, I saw three milk-pale, cloven hemispheres of the girls' derrières, as they suddenly stopped in knee-high water.

Ripping all my clothes off, I ran after them and saw Madeleine look back and reach her hand out to me. "The water's cold," she said, as I took her hand. I fixed my eyes on her face and tried to internalize that finally, for the first time in my life, I was in the presence of a totally naked woman . . . who wasn't my mother. What's more, a woman who wasn't trying to hide her nakedness from me.

Surges of heat rushed through my body. I didn't dare take my eyes from Madeleine's round face and felt incredible gratitude for the gift which she was bestowing on me.

I wanted to look down, but I didn't need to. The mere fact that she was standing there in front of me like that was everything. Were my emotions not already committed to Susan, I would have raised Madeleine's soft hand in both of mine and kissed her little fingers tenderly.

Then, from one of the other girls I heard a whispered, "Look at Mr. Padowiczki," and was embarrassed to find that my own naked flesh was giving away my inner excitement.

"Come on!" Madeleine said again. Letting go of the other girl, she began to run into deeper water, pulling me with her. We were treading the cold water, and I was glad that the water on my face hid my tears of gratitude.

Madeleine put her hands on my two shoulders and said, "It's all right, Mr. Padowicz," in a voice as sweet as an angel's. Oh my god! What I wouldn't have given for the freedom to pull her against me and wrap my aching arms around her.

Chapter Sixteen

With so much in New York to attract my attention, I took little notice of changes that were taking place in the Szyk household. Unbeknownst to me at the time, Uncle Arthur's hatred of tyranny had brought him into conflict with Senator Joseph McCarthy and his committee investigating "un-American activities." Whether my uncle had actually attacked the tyranny of the McCarthy Committee directly through his art, as he well may have, I didn't know, but a year or so earlier in retaliation for something or other the committee had launched an investigation into his loyalty. And, like the writers and filmmakers whose loyalty the committee was also investigating, my uncle had found the demand for his work suddenly drying up. The prestigious commercial clients whose magazine advertisements he had been producing became fearful of the guilt-by-association pandemic that the committee was smearing across America the way rats had spread the Black Death over fourteenth-century Europe.

Uncle Arthur was no businessman. His income was all invested in the good fellowship that his beautiful New Canaan home provided to his family and his legions of friends. Now the income was gone. Suddenly the dinner parties and the holiday celebrations had come to an end and the servants were released with liberal compensation.

Aunt Julia sat me down at some point and explained that belts would have to be tightened, and that we would all have to pitch in to help. Since I already had lawn-mowing responsibilities on the ten-acre estate and provided chauffeuring services when called upon, I did not see my burden increasing significantly. However, the sight of Cousin Alice or her sister-in-law, Collette, guiding the Hoover over the oriental rug in the living room brought to mind thoughts of Chekhov's *Cherry Orchard*, which I had studied that past year.

But I could find no literary parallel to apply to Aunt Julia's taking driving lessons. The clutch-to-accelerator relationship of their standard-shift 1946 Chevrolet was a mystery my aunt never did master, much to the merriment of us all and, particularly, my aged grandmother, who was the only person who would ever ride with her. "I have little to lose," she explained to me.

I knew that my mother was paying generously for my and Grandmother's keep, but I didn't know to what extent cousins Alice and George might be contributing. Alice's husband, Joe, had a diamond import business that I knew wasn't going well, and George, trained in the law at the Sorbonne in Paris before going into the army, could not practice in America and was now a stockbroker with a New York firm. But the little time that he actually spent in New York was a subject of considerable humor in the household whenever he left for the tennis court.

Humor was one thing that did not seem to diminish. Uncle Arthur had imbued us all with humor as the default response to adversity, and gloom didn't stand a chance. I remember his asking me one time to park my eleven-year-old, bailing wire-and-chewing gum–secured Dodge in back of the house because he didn't want visitors "thinking we had poor relatives." We both laughed at the irony in his statement and it remains in my memory as my most intimate moment with my uncle.

With the house finally still at night, isolated by the dark and with the day's bustle dropping away into the quiet, I would sometimes find myself suddenly in tears over the tragedy of it all—my Uncle Arthur, whose art had been a battle flag through the world war, who had thrashed brutality and intolerance according to his own high principles and the American ideal as espoused by the statesmen and teachers throughout the nation, had suddenly been rejected and abandoned beside the road by his adopted country. How he could maintain his good humor in the face of this betrayal was beyond me.

But Uncle Arthur had not been idle. He had taken on a speculative project. He proceeded to illuminate the Declaration of Independence as he had other historic documents. This, however, was not to be reproduced on commission, but at his own expense and marketed for profit. It is a stunning piece of work, thirty-five inches by twenty-eight, many times larger than his standard paintings, and full of beautiful detail. Today, his original hangs in the Library of Congress and I find reproductions decorating classrooms and government offices.

Near the end of the summer, I was awakened by hurried footsteps outside my room. My aunt and uncle had returned from a dinner party some hours earlier and retired. Alice and Joe were now in New York, where nine-year-old Katherine would be starting school, and George and Colette had gone to bed before I had.

Stepping out onto the landing, I found the lights on in my aunt and uncle's bedroom and a man leaning over the bed. Uncle Arthur was in the bed, naked with a sheet covering his lower body.

I recognized the visitor as Dr. Rosenack, a friend of the Szyks. He instructed me to go out into the street to direct the police and the ambulance up our driveway when they arrived. I pulled on my clothes and ran down the driveway.

The police and the ambulance arrived in short order. When I had followed them back up to the house, Aunt Julia and Dr. Rosenack's wife were sitting downstairs in the library.

"Any news?" my aunt asked.

I said that the police and the ambulance had arrived.

"Go up and find out," she urged.

Upstairs, uniformed men were standing around Uncle Arthur's bed. George was kneeling on the bed, holding an oxygen mask to his father's face. "Breathe, father," he was saying in English, which struck me as odd, as they normally conversed in Polish.

"Tell Julia to come back upstairs quickly," Dr. Rosenack instructed me.

I ran back down and returned with my aunt. I stood back as she stepped around the bed to my uncle's head and began whispering to him in Polish.

"Breathe, father," George kept saying.

Then there was a strange sound, and my uncle became still. He didn't move again. His heart had finally broken.

Chapter Seventeen

The Colgate Commons Club ate their lunches and dinners downtown, at the bar-with-a-restaurant called the Old Stone Jug. As a freshman, my meals at the student union had been paid for in advance. Over the summer I had asked my mother not to pay for any more student union meals but to give the money to me instead so that I could eat with my fraternity brothers. Had I joined a Greek letter fraternity, I reminded her, there would have been considerably bigger costs.

I had watched Mother turn to Pierre to ask if he thought I was telling the truth or whether this was some trick. "He spends money like a sailor, you know."

I had no history of not telling Mother the truth or trying to trick her or of having large sums of money to spend, but I can't say that I was all that surprised at her reaction. With me sitting not ten feet away, Pierre conceded that what I said sounded reasonable. I then explained, as I had before, that textbooks had to be purchased as well and that there were other expenses along the way.

I came back to school with five twenty-dollar bills in my pocket. I had said that it would not be enough, but Mother said to call her when I ran out and "We'll see."

I managed my money very carefully. Commons Club dues could be delayed by a few weeks, and books I didn't know what to do with anyway. Food, however, was of the essence.

Riding down the hill into town with my brothers for meals was a new and very pleasant experience. Most of the Jug's business was in the bar, patronized by Hamilton's agricultural residents. The restaurant was in a separate room with four booths, a coin-operated table shuffleboard, and a cash register. It was presided over by Alice, the thirty-something daughter of the bar's owners who had a withered arm, knew the brothers by name, shared jokes with us, listened to our troubles, and served from a very limited menu. It wasn't much, but it was home.

I was surprised that there weren't more of us there and discovered that many Commons Clubbers worked for their meals and part of their tuition at the student union. I was glad that Mother had not heard of this option—I did not relish washing dishes and cleaning tables after herds of freshmen. And the pleasure of being one of the guys at the Stone Jug was powerful.

My previous year's roommate, Raza, who had pledged the club with me, had also joined the Outing Club and urged me to join with him. I would have enjoyed the activity, but there were expenses involved and I had to decline. But in spite of my skimping, in a few weeks I was down to three days' worth of food money.

I called Mother. "I'm so glad you called," she said. "I just thought of something wonderful for you."

I automatically cringed.

"You know that song I like to sing?" Then she sang the five words and some *la la las* of a French song I had heard her sing before. The five words translated to, "And the little white wines."

"Yes, I do."

"Wouldn't it be a wonderful sight if all the boys marched down the hill to class every morning singing that song?"

I knew what was coming next, and I couldn't believe what I was hearing. I made some sound that I thought would please Mother.

"Well, you should teach them all to sing it," she said.

I searched my brain for the reason she might most readily accept. "I don't know the words," I finally said.

"Well, you know," and she sang her five words again.

I presented reality as gently as I could. "That's only five words."

"Oh, but think what a wonderful scene it will be, the whole college marching down that beautiful hill to class, singing a French song. Like in that movie."

I immediately recalled a scene in *How Green Was My Valley*, where the Welsh miners walk home from the mines singing and could see how that would be attractive to Mother.

"You know the one," Mother said, "*Snow White*."

With Welsh coalminers now replaced in my mind by bearded diamond-miner dwarves, I said, "I'll see what I can do."

"Oh Julian, you're such a wimp. Say, 'I *will* do it. It might be difficult, but *I will find a way*.' That's the only way to succeed in life."

I could not deny that I lacked the expected aggressiveness. "I have a problem," I murmured.

"Always he has a problem," Mother said.

"I'm almost out of money."

"We gave you a hundred dollars."

"The cheapest item on the menu is three dollars and twenty-five cents."

"Money, money, money. We will come, not this weekend but the next, and straighten it out for you." Then she hung up.

Bizarre as the conversation had been, I could not help feeling that my mother would have found a way to teach a certain number of my fellow Colgate students to sing that silly song, walking down the hill (classes were on top of the hill), even with the *la la las*. As that night's darkness cut through the protection of my not-totally-disproven hypothesis, I could hear ineffectual little Julian whimpering not far below me.

The next day I went to the student aid office to apply for a job. Campus jobs, I learned, were in short supply. In addition, your parents had to file a certificate of financial need. There was no way that was going to happen for me.

I went to the grocery store and invested my remaining money in cans of Campbell's soup. I didn't have enough for a hotplate. Fortunately I knew that one of the brothers had one, and I managed on tomato soup for the next week and a half until my parents arrived. That I was still walking and talking when they arrived, I considered a victory.

"Mrs. Malden says that her son lives in a fraternity where they have a cook, and he doesn't have to pay anything," Mother said through the car window, when they arrived. "Why do you have to pay?"

"We don't have a kitchen," I explained. "And I'm sure that Mrs. Malden pays a boarding fee considerably greater than what I need."

"Why don't you live in one of those nice fraternity houses with a kitchen?" she asked.

"Because they discriminate against Negroes and Jews," I said, "and I don't want to belong to such a fraternity."

"You didn't tell them you are Jewish?" she suddenly demanded.

"No, I did not. I just don't want to belong to a fraternity that discriminates against anybody." And suddenly I knew that it was possible to be proud and ashamed at the same time. I was proud of the statement I had just made and ashamed that it was all a fat lie. Remarkably, the fact that I, myself, might have been the victim of such discrimination never entered my mind. My personal inadequacies, I knew, were sufficient to keep me off any list of desirable candidates for membership.

We drove to the Inn where Mother could get a cup of coffee and Pierre a Scotch and soda. Then Mother wanted to see where I spent my food money. I took her around the corner to the Old Stone Jug and introduced her to Alice. Then I watched in disbelief as Mother gave her name and address to the young woman. They would charge all my meals and send the bill to Mother. I felt a huge, huge stone roll off my chest.

What this meant was that I would be free of begging Mother for food money, I could have desserts, and I could, sometimes, have a glass of beer—even buy an occasional beer for a brother. And it meant that when Susan came for party weekend, I could feed her for free.

It was in my sophomore year that I first encountered Professor Kistler. Jonathan Hipperling Kistler taught a course called "The Novel," certainly a must for an aspiring writer.

He looked to be in his fifties with steel-gray hair that stood straight up, reminding me of a comical movie character of a few years earlier named the Mad Russian. He had a little mustache as well, and when asked a question he would put the fingertips of one hand to his lower lip, his head tilted slightly back, and think out his answer. If the question provoked enough thought, the fingertips of both hands would come together to rest on his mustache, and you could almost hear the switches in his brain snapping open and closed, shunting electrons this way and that. And the fact that a question of mine could put all that thinking apparatus into motion gave me a whole new sensation of worth.

At first I had felt uncomfortable putting the man to such trouble. Had I known the answer was not readily available to him I would not have dared to bother the poor man. But I came to realize that Professor Kistler never gave readily available answers. If you asked him how the weather was, he would wonder if that might be because you had no raincoat for the trip down the hill for lunch. And if you asked him for the time, you might get a story about an uncle, back on the farm, who could never wear a watch because his body's magnetic force field would magnetize the works and cause them to jam.

Professor Kistler liked to ask questions in class. With one foot on the table in front of him, he would perch there like a raptor ready to rip the responses from his students. If you had no response to a question about Hans Castorp's motivation or Emma Bovary's attitude, by the time you had responded to his narrower, subsequent questions, you realized that you actually did have that desired response and, furthermore, that you were a genius to have it. And, sitting there among juniors and seniors, as well as fellow sophomores, I had the strong feeling that I was one of the brightest, if not *the* brightest of the geniuses in his class.

Never before had I felt myself among the brighter students in any class. It was only, I believed, my freak ability to screw words together in interesting sequences that enabled my indolent, unacademic mind to occupy space at an institution of higher learning.

I took as many of Professor Kistler's courses as I could over the next three years, including Shakespeare. There were other teachers in the English department, some with prestigious names in academia, but with none did I feel as anything but my usual dumb self. It was only Professor Kistler who was somehow able to see the glimmer of perception buried under layers of I-don't-know-what inside me and bring it out to where I could see it as well.

One day I brought him a short story I had recently written. As I left his slit of an office in Lawrence Hall, I could see Mr. Kistler leaning back in his squeaky tilting chair, his foot against the pull of a desk drawer, my story in his hand, the eraser end of a pencil against his lower lip. "Come back in an hour," he had said, though it couldn't have taken more than fifteen minutes to read the story.

I sat on the hallway floor outside Professor Kistler's office for precisely sixty minutes. When I returned, he was still holding my manuscript and told me it was the best undergraduate story he had ever read. When I asked if I should go on writing, he said, "Oh yes. You'll be a writer some day."

I would take several more courses with Professor Kistler and, after my graduation, his family and I would become close friends. We would exchange visits and I would, eventually, have the sad honor of speaking at his memorial service.

That I was able to advance from one year to the next despite my inability to study was a bit of a mystery to me. At first I had sincerely tried to complete my reading assignments but there just were not enough hours in the night for me to read every line. And as to knowing what I had read, my mind was much too occupied with the mechanics of reading and the frustration of the entire process to concern itself with content.

What I did do, and this was not in conscious compensation but simply because it seemed to be my nature, was ask a lot of questions in class and push my way into many class discussions. Many of the professors and instructors took umbrage at this. They thought I was arguing, that I was trying to trip them up. Nothing could have been further from the truth. Confrontation was not my style. I just found that by asking, "Does that mean that . . . ?" possibly several times in succession, I could narrow the focus down to the nucleus that gave me a sudden grasp of the entire subject.

On more than one occasion, an annoyed teacher would demand, "Mr. Padowicz, have you even been listening to what I've been saying?" at which point I would repeat his entire lecture back to him. While my final grades were rarely above a "gentleman C," my in-class questioning, bolstered by the high grades I managed to earn on my written assignments, somehow got me through.

Returning from one weekend with Susan, I was told by my roommates that I had missed my parents' visit. My phone call to Montreal discovered an outraged Mother. "Everyone was there, except for you! How could you?"

"How could you possibly know whether everyone was there or not?"

"Pierre and I went to look for you at the place where you drink beer on weekends, and the whole school was there except you."

"The whole school would not fit in that pub. But, if you had told me you were coming, I would certainly have waited for you."

"We couldn't tell you we were coming because we didn't know. But the weather was so nice on Saturday morning, so we thought we'd pop in and visit you, but you weren't there."

"I appreciate that, but you know that I spend a lot of my weekends in Massachusetts. You should have let me know."

"The whole school was there. We had no idea you'd be gone."

"I'm sorry you came down for nothing."

"Oh, we didn't come down for nothing. We had a good time with all your friends. You were the only one who wasn't there."

Mother had some friends in Westport, a town some twenty minutes from the Szyks' home in New Canaan. The man's name was Leopold Godowsky Jr., and he had been a concert violinist who, along with fellow musician Leopold Mannes, had developed the first marketable color film, Kodachrome. His wife was the former Frances Gershwin, sister of the late composer George Gershwin. They had a pretty daughter my age named Sandra, and Mother arranged that we meet.

I liked Sandra. She was pretty, funny, and fun to be with, but there was one big problem—Sandra liked me *a lot*. She laughed at my unfunny, inappropriate humor, implying to me that despite her lineage, pretty Sandra did not have Susan's discretion. She didn't know bad humor or clumsy behavior when she saw them.

I saw Sandra a number of times and, at Mother's insistence, even took her to a dance. We had a good time together. We actually had more to talk about and considerably more fun talking about it than I did with Susan. But I knew that anyone who perceived me in any light other than the harsh reality by which Susan and my mother held me could not have been very bright.

There was a small complication before my sophomore year ended. One evening at the end of our dinner at the Old Stone Jug, Alice called me into the next room and informed me quietly that Mother had not paid any of my food bills.

Alice had written her several times, she said, but had never received an answer.

That Mother could ignore my concerns was no news to me. But that she might be derelict in her business dealings with other adults had never entered my mind. I recalled her on that train to Reno, in her filmy nightgown and bare feet confronting the conductor over his lack of patriotism. I thought of the woman who, barely speaking English, had marched into the offices of a New York publisher and come out with a book contract and an advance. And I, of course, remembered her in her fur coat turned inside out in her awkward impersonation of a peasant woman, trudging through the snow over the Carpathian Mountains on her gimpy leg and telling me not to worry because mothers had a special sense of direction. That my concern over a few dollars for textbooks might not register as imperative in her scale of values, I could understand. But that she would shirk a commitment she had made to another adult did not . . . well, in today's terms we would say, "It just didn't compute."

I asked Alice to show me the address she had mailed the bills to. Had she failed to write *Canada* on the envelope? Had she, perhaps, put insufficient postage on the envelope? The Peel Street address in Montreal, PQ, Canada, that Alice showed me in her notebook was totally correct. And she had taken the letters to the post office herself and had them weighed by the postal employee. I could not imagine what could have gone wrong.

I called Mother that evening and explained the mysterious problem. Yes, she admitted, that awful little woman with the club foot had been pestering her for payment. Yes, she would certainly pay my little bill, but on her own schedule.

As far as I was concerned, the operative word in that conversation was *awful.* That Mother should apply that adjective to Alice, presumably because she was a waitress and because she had a withered arm which Mother remembered as a club foot, stunned me and stung me to the core of my sensibilities. If anything, Alice should be pitied for her disability, except that she didn't ask for pity. Alice was our big sister who laughed at our jokes, advised us on our girlfriend problems, and sneaked an extra meatball into our spaghetti. Mother had been careful not to make any negative remarks about Susan's social background in my presence, though I was sure she entertained them. But to attack Alice in this vicious manner . . .

I had no words to respond with. I hung up the receiver.

In the summer following my sophomore year, Susan and I decided to attend the summer program at Tufts together. I signed up for a course in Greek drama and one in modern poetry. Majoring in government, Susan took something else. She also worked a few hours a week at the library for a modest stipend, and I got a local laundry and dry cleaner to let me be their pickup and delivery man on campus on a commission basis. We would meet for lunch and dinner and in the evenings.

Having experienced one trip between Montreal and Hamilton in my 1940 Dodge with its slippery clutch and asthmatic motor, Mother had decided that summer that someone who covered the miles that I did between Hamilton, Medford, Montreal, and New Canaan needed a suitable vehicle. Most likely with money from Reggie Purbrick, she surprised me with a brand new Plymouth. In addition, somewhere along the line someone had convinced her that a young college man needed cash in his pocket, and now for the first time in my life I had a modest allowance, which my dry cleaner's job augmented.

It was the first time since Hudson Camp when I was ten that I was living on a co-ed campus, the first time since the day school on Riverside Drive that there were girls attending class with me, the first time that passing a woman in the hall didn't prompt turning to watch her walk away. It was the first time that a woman who smiled a greeting at me in the library wasn't already somebody else's date for the weekend.

Well aware of my inexperience in these matters, Susan was not stingy with her tutelage. She let me know when it had been reported to her that I had walked out of the bookstore talking with Helen or explained my understanding of Antigone's motivation to Irene following Greek drama class. It was not that these acts were in themselves improper, she assured me, it was just that I needed to know that she was aware of them. I considered myself informed.

I had a radio in my new car, and now, sixty years later, I still remember the songs that we heard that summer. Nat King Cole was walking his baby back home, Jo Stafford admonished me that when a dream appeared I was to remember that I belong to her, and a Cajun woman sang that she was going to have a good time on the bayou and that kinfolk came by the dozen to see her John . . . or was it john?

One Saturday, Susan signed out of her dorm for the weekend and we drove to Cape Cod, two hours away. I had never been to Cape Cod but Susan had and, she informed me, there was a town called Provincetown where homosexuals hung out. The word *gay* had not come into common usage yet. I had never seen a homosexual, as far as I knew. I had a vague idea of what it was they did, though I was baffled by the mechanics of it. Once inside the Provincetown limits, we looked at every pedestrian we passed but could not say that we saw anything worth the trip. We had pizza and beer for supper, exhausting our pooled funds, and with two blankets we had brought from our dorms we found a secluded spot among the dunes for the night.

There was no confusion about the mechanics available to the two of us, if we dared to avail ourselves of them. But that kind of mechanics too often resulted in babies, and we weren't about to risk that. Still, with the intimacy we achieved that night I realized that my commitment to Susan was now complete. Comfortable or uncomfortable as I might be with her surveillance of my activities in the bookstore, my honor was now pledged totally to Susan.

Mother had requested that for the last week of summer vacation I come visit them in Montreal. After driving Susan home to New Canaan, I headed my blue Plymouth northward along Route 9.

One evening, Pierre was demonstrating with his cane the saber thrusts and slashes he had learned in cavalry school, and I mentioned that I would have liked to learn the sport of fencing myself.

"Why don't you go down to the YMCA and see if they give fencing instruction?" Pierre suggested, and the following day I did just that. Two days later I had my first fencing lesson, for which Pierre had prepared me by explaining the difference between a foil, an epée, and a saber. He further explained that there were two categories of foil, each requiring its own technique, the French and the Italian, of which the French was far superior.

In that one lesson I learned to hold a French foil; to advance, retreat, thrust, and lunge; and to perform several parries. The school term began before I could have a second lesson but to my delight I discovered in the catalog that Colgate offered fencing instruction as part of the physical education program. I signed up for the course and showed up eagerly for class.

There were five or six other students waiting with me but the instructor did not appear. Then the director of physical education came into the room and informed us that, regrettably, the instructor would not be able to teach the class. "Does anyone here know how to fence?" he asked.

No hands went up.

"Does anyone here know *anything* about fencing?" he asked again.

I raised my hand halfway. "I took some instruction at the Y," I said.

"Then would you like to teach the course?"

I said that well, yes, I would.

"You'll be paid forty-five cents an hour. Come into my office after class and give your name to my secretary."

That same afternoon I went to the library and checked out every book they had on the subject of fencing. Surprisingly, I had no trouble assimilating what I read in these texts. Two days later I taught my new students how to take the *en garde* position and to advance and retreat, holding the other elements for future classes. I continued to teach fencing at forty-five cents an hour for my remaining two years at Colgate.

Chapter Eighteen

My job teaching fencing for two hours a week gave me
a sense of self-esteem—I was an instructor. Not only
was I an instructor, but I was one who had parlayed the
position on the basis of having received only one lesson
at the Montreal YMCA. There was a certain panache
to that.

I had an idea for enlarging my prestige. Within a half
hour's drive there was the women's institution named
Cazenovia Junior College where on a Friday or Saturday
night a Colgate man could walk into a dorm and find a
companion for a walk to the Caz Bar for a few friendly
beers. Betting that the college didn't have its own fencing
instructor, I came up with a plan.

My commitment to Susan prevented me from availing
myself of the above accommodation, but there was a reason behind my plan. I surprised Raza, my freshman-year
roommate and now my fraternity brother, by suggesting
that we drive to Cazenovia and buy a couple of girls a
couple of beers. Since Raza didn't have a car of his own,
he thought my plan a good one.

I don't remember the name of my date that night or
what she looked like. What I do remember, however, is
what we talked about. We talked about the fact that Cazenovia did not have a fencing program and about how I

should go about offering my services for an evening's demonstration of this sport.

The following week I was on the phone with the appropriate faculty person, and it was arranged that on a certain evening I would come and give a demonstration to whatever students were interested. On the appointed evening I showed up, foil in hand, wearing a fencing jacket, to face a gym full of enthusiastic young women.

I explained the difference between the foil, the epée, and the saber, as well as between the French and Italian foils. I demonstrated the *en garde* position, the advance, retreat, thrust, lunge, parry, and riposte. I asked for volunteers to try the various moves. With the side of my blade I touched a leg that wasn't totally extended, an arm that might have dropped too low, or a foot that wasn't at the full ninety degrees.

For a full hour or so I held the undivided attention of several dozen enthusiastic young women. When my demonstration was over I received generous applause, and as I prepared to leave one member of the faculty slipped me two twenty dollar bills. I did not get to sleep till very early the next morning, nor was there a single whimper from Julian.

I did not make strong friendships at Colgate. I was friendly, I liked people, and on a one-to-one basis I could get along with almost anyone. But I wasn't yet ready for male bonding. My greatest needs were self-appreciation and the tender love of a woman. And with Susan, who I knew had more important things in her life, I could at least pretend.

My fraternity brothers were appreciative of the ideas I came up with for displays in front of our dorm before football games and of my willingness to construct them, but what do you do with that? The guys that I took to Massachusetts and fixed up with dates because I wanted com-

pany on the long drives were usually too bleary-eyed when
we returned to express much appreciation, and they never
invited me to anything in return. I was pleasant enough
company, but whatever a young man might need from a
close friend I knew that I didn't have to offer. I might be
of some use to my fraternity brothers for attracting other
pledges, and I might occasionally luck into something like
my fencing instructor position, but clearly something was
missing from my character.

Even my very Commons Club membership caused
me grief on sleepless nights. While Groucho Marx had
declared that any club that wanted him as a member he
desired no part of, I had shown no such discretion and
gone ahead and joined. The fact that the Commons Club
regularly outscored all other fraternities in the academic
grades department and that it contained many campus
leaders was negatively offset by the knowledge that they
had been able to find no better freshman to "build" their
"pledge class around" than my worthless self.

That Susan found me acceptable was the crown jewel of
my life. The word *love* never passed between us anymore.
I had tried using it a few times but Susan informed me
that what I was feeling was not love but infatuation, and
she knew more about these things than I did. *Infatuation*
I knew to be a polite term for a man's chemical need to
invade a woman's person. Because it was a chemical need,
it was not in itself evil. What was evil, and what I was fully
guilty of, was the inability to suppress that need.

It was astounding that Susan tolerated my lack of control, that she would allow my hands to "accidently" come
into contact with her sacred places. As, with the passage of
time, I found Susan even loosening her clothing in preparation for our front-seat acrobatics, I understood that despite
her reluctance to articulate it she must, indeed, love me.

I could imagine no other reason for an honorable young woman to allow such invasion of her person. And the belief that Susan returned my nefarious infatuation with true love, I treasured above all else in my life.

It did not worry me that Susan did not respond to my daily letters with equal frequency. I did not like it, but who was I to expect better? I knew that she studied for her classes while I only pretended to. But when weeks went by without a letter, despite my explanations to myself for the void I would grow anxious and look for ways to dispel that anxiety.

I finally found it in tennis. Not the tennis team, because I didn't believe myself to be a good enough player even to be considered. And not playing with a friend, because that required cultivating a tennis friend. The far easier path was to go down the hill to the gym in the evening and hit a ball against the tiled wall.

This, I reasoned, was a constructive activity. The ability to play good tennis could be a serious asset in one's adult career. And while I had never had a tennis lesson, I further reasoned that with enough repetitions I would discover, through trial and error, the correct way to grip a racquet and to meet the ball for the greatest effect.

And this activity had another, totally unexpected result. With my mind's natural inclination to wander away from the subject at hand, I soon found myself thinking not of ball-hitting mechanics but story ideas. And as an idea developed in my head, I did not need to feel guilty and try to return to my book but I could let my tennis strokes grow sluggish while my mind raced through various plot developments until I found myself standing there, the racquet hanging by my side. Then I would run up the hill to my room to put it all on paper.

Unfortunately there was nothing I could do with my short stories. Strangely, Colgate had only one creative writing course, and I had taken that already. It was a seminar that met once a week to read our stories to each other and suffer the comments. And my peers had not cheered my writing universally. The statement, "I don't get it," would often be applied, only not as an apology but rather as an accusation.

Colgate had a literary magazine, but the thought of some student editor rejecting my submission because its literary values were over his head and giving his preference to some other student's lame attempt presented a risk my ego could not take. To shatter my image of literary superiority would have lowered me to the ranks, a level at which I could not compete.

One day, my Czechoslovakian fraternity brother, Raza, a philosophy major, introduced me to a story entitled "Tobermory" by someone named Saki. This writer, whom I took to be Japanese but later learned was an Englishman named H. H. Munro, had written about a talking cat named Tobermory who raised hell in a proper English household by repeating the various secrets that had been said in its presence.

The wit with which this story was told captivated me. I remembered some of the writings of James Thurber and E. B. White that I had enjoyed at Millbrook and suddenly immersed myself in satire. I read every bit of humor that I could lay my hands on and judged it harshly by some standards I had established, mostly based on subtlety.

Then I began writing my own satire. My favorite from those days is a story about a professor of literature who raises a baby chimpanzee. Somewhere I had read the theory that given enough chimpanzees banging randomly on enough typewriters, in sufficient time they will have pounded out copies of all of the world's great literature. Extending this hyperbola I had this chimpanzee pounding out original literature from the very start. The literary world marveled at this phenomenon, but a member of the United States Senate discovered a vein of communistic philosophy running through his work and the typewriter had to be taken away. I don't remember the story's ending but it was not a happy one for either the professor or his chimp.

I dared not show these stories to anyone who might not admire them. Leading that list was Professor Kistler, whose classical tastes might not appreciate my satire. I did, however, have a serious short story, reminiscent of Ring Lardner, which I again had the courage to show him. Because it was a Friday when I delivered it to his office, Professor Kistler suggested that I come to his house the following day for my critique.

Arriving at the professor's house a half mile from the campus, I was met at the door by a young woman my own age in shorts and bare feet who introduced herself as Tasha, Professor Kistler's daughter. It did not take a genius to realize that Tasha's actual name must be Natasha, after Tolstoy's young heroine in *War and Peace*.

"I liked your story," she informed me as she let me into the house. It turned out that her mother had read and liked it as well. Then, as we drank coffee and ate homemade coffee cake while waiting for Professor Kistler to return from the post office, I found myself answering questions about the young man who was the hero of my story.

Sitting there and discussing characters I had invented, I could not help wishing that I could have conversations like that with Susan. I could not help wishing that Susan and my future mother-in-law moved around their own home dispensing homemade coffee cake as easily and gracefully as these two. And then, when Tasha's father returned and praised my story as well and the four of us went on to discuss other stories and other authors, I found myself overcome by a great sadness as I realized that I was committed to a life that would not contain such pleasures.

It is a highly cherished tradition for students to attach nicknames to their instructors and, as instructor of fencing, I was no exception. Just two years earlier, José Ferrer had received an Oscar for portraying the freak-nosed swordsman/poet Cyrano de Bergerac and my students did not let this resemblance go unnoticed. I had seen the film as well and taken great pride in the hero's "Magnificent, my nose" speech. I did not, of course, dare to tell Mother about this comparison.

I didn't have to. Whenever Mother's hand came to her face in some gesture of inner pain while looking at me, I knew she was thinking of my nose. The bounty on that part of my anatomy had gone up to five thousand dollars, but I still refused. "Do it for me, darling, please. Show me how much you love me," she would plead, and I would shake my head.

One day, Mother took a different tack. There was just a slight hesitation of indecision as she first addressed me, but then I could see her make the decision and plow ahead. "Yulian, you just don't realize how ugly you look," Mother said in Polish.

I knew very well what I looked like and Mother's self-serving words could have no effect on my self-image. Appearance was not my major problem. What her statement did have an effect—a profound effect—on was my image of her. Even naïve as I was in these matters, I realized that those words of hers had stepped over a line. What parent said that kind of thing to a child, unless she was trying to inflict damage? And Mother, I knew, was not really trying to damage me—or was she?

But what I now recognized was that the mother who had led me over the Carpathian Mountains, who had marched into the publisher's office with a book proposal, who had upbraided that train conductor, simply knew no bounds in pursuit of her will. In pursuit of her chosen goal, Mother would face any danger and inflict any damage necessary to fulfill that objective.

I looked to Pierre, my stepfather, who had come out of the war with an artificial leg, medals, and a dream to accompany General de Gaulle in putting right their country's inefficient and corrupt political system, who had the war record and the charisma for a brilliant political career but who was, instead, a poorly paid, minor functionary in a small consulate because Mother had wanted to be a diplomat's wife. I remembered my first stepfather, Lolek, whom I could visualize being notified by the Red Cross in his prisoner of war camp that his wife had just divorced him. And I recalled the scandals associated with my own father's suicide and suddenly realized what a minefield I was standing in. I realized that my mother had the ability to damage lives and that she had the will to use that power, that she had already damaged mine through the nurturing she had denied me, through the multitude of embarrassing and impossible situations I had been placed in.

But, unlike Pierre, whose Scotch and sodas were considerably denser in color now than they had once been, who now managed to refill his glass more often, whose nose and cheeks were beginning to show the broken veins of liver damage, whose meager earnings were periodically augmented by Reggie Purbrick's largesse, and with whom my discussions of world affairs too often now ended with his mumbling, "The only good thing in America is the cigarettes," I had survived. I was still standing, I was still involved with the girl of my own choosing and, figuratively speaking, at least, I still wore Cyrano's white plume of independence.

Chapter Nineteen

Parting from Susan to return to Colgate for the start of my junior year had a different flavor. I knew that I was up against a reality I could not cover with my often-helpful hypothesis regarding believing your way to success. A year ahead of me in school, Susan would be graduating that coming spring. Having majored in government, she planned to go to Washington to begin a career in government service. This was reality. Once she moved to Washington and went to work in Congress or one of the agencies, a popular girl like Susan would get swallowed up in that way of life, and I would surely lose her. Forlorn little Julian was, again, sniveling in my bed.

I would, of course, be free then to court the attractive and friendly Tasha Kistler. But how responsive would Tasha be to Julian's advances? While under different circumstances I might have rated my chances with Tasha as pretty good, in this realistic moment I was positive that fate would not treat me well. Extended exposure would certainly convince the well-bred Sandra Godowsky that I was not who she took me to be. And I would be alone again.

The solution was marriage.

Just off campus Colgate maintained a collection of housing units we called Vetville. It was a cluster of small apartments built quickly at the end of the war to accommodate the married veterans taking advantage of the GI Bill of Rights to get a free education. The bulk of those veterans were long graduated, and now the housing was available to any married students or faculty for a very modest rent. Susan and I could live there during my senior year. When I graduated I would receive a second lieutenant's commission in the air force and earn officers' pay for the next three years.

Only two details needed to be dealt with in order to put this plan into action. One was for Susan to say yes; the other was for my mother to give or to lend me the small amount of cash that life in Vetville would cost above what she was already paying for my room and board. Susan, who had worked part-time at the Tufts library the summer before, could do so at Colgate and maybe even get a secretarial job with the university.

Susan's approval was surprisingly easy. It turned out that she had assumed that we would marry following my own graduation. My plan only meant advancing the date by a year. I suspect that her mother also much preferred this route over seeing her daughter off to Washington. As to my own mother, that was a different situation.

I had noticed, over the past year or so, that Mother and Pierre's financial situation seemed to have improved considerably, which was encouraging. My new car and the allowance I was now receiving signaled some kind of change. Perhaps some settlement had been made with Reggie Purbrick; maybe he had passed away and mentioned Mother in his will. I didn't know.

What I did know was that I held one bargaining chip. Or rather that a bargaining chip grew at the end of my nose. The last quote of its market value had been five thousand dollars. Five thousand additional dollars would get Susan and me by quite well.

I drove to Montreal during mid-winter break prepared to put my Cyrano nose on the block. Driving to Montreal in the middle of winter was chancy, but the weather turned out to be on my side.

"We would move to a larger apartment," Mother explained when I arrived, "but Pierre is about to be promoted and transferred to Philadelphia."

Her candid and unsolicited explanation surprised me. Explaining her plans to me had never been Mother's style. She may have sensed my surprise because she reminded me that I had turned twenty-one since my last visit, and she evidently considered that a significant milestone in our relationship. I was glad to hear this because it would, I expected, make my request easier to negotiate.

Then Mother sat me down on the sofa and seated herself beside me. "I have something very important to tell you," she said. She had switched to Polish, which she used when she didn't want Pierre to understand. Pierre, however, was still at the office.

Then to my seven-year-old's Polish vocabulary was added the word for *affair*. It seemed that Mother wanted me to know that she had had an affair. "Now that you are twenty-one I can be telling you this," she reminded me again. I had no wish to share this intimacy.

I did not understand. That Mother must have used sex to achieve her goals over the years was something that I had come to assume. As I looked back at our adventurous progress from Soviet-occupied Poland to where we were, it became clear to me once I was old enough to understand these things that Mother had used every weapon at her disposal. It certainly wasn't something I would condemn her for. Why she would have the need to tell me this now

would have baffled me except for the fact that nothing that
Mother did baffled me anymore.

But Mother continued. She gave the name of the man
with whom she had had this affair and was surprised I did
not recognize it. "Yulian, you have to know these things,"
she admonished. Whether she was referring to the story
she was unfolding or the evident significance of the name
she had just revealed, I did not know. "He and his brother
own—" and she went on to name a corporation I did
recognize.

If she wanted me to be impressed by her liaison, then
my being impressed could put me in a better bargaining
position. I made a face that I hoped implied my being
very impressed.

But Mother wasn't finished. Now I learned another Polish word, the word for *blackmail.* It seemed that Mother
further wanted me to know that she was blackmailing the
gentleman to the tune of five thousand dollars a month,
a princely sum in 1953.

"We are still friends," she continued. "He lives right here
on Peel Street and five thousand dollars is nothing to him.
And I, of course, have no need to tell anybody, so we are
still friends. You will meet him. You should know this."

Why I should know this continued to elude me. I wondered where Pierre thought this influx of money came
from. I remembered Mother marching to show off her
Russian to Dr. Parry over my objections, urging Pierre
to upbraid me over my car in Dean Kalgrin's office, and
calling me ugly. I felt no pain, but neither did I feel any
empathy. And it was then that a diabolical plan formed
itself in my mind. Never mind my poor maligned nose, I
had a better card to play. And it had nothing to do with
her blackmailing scheme.

"You know that Susan is due to graduate at the end of this year," I said, after a suitable pause. Mother admitted that she hadn't known that.

"Well, she will and she plans to go to find a job in Washington."

"Why all the way to Washington?" Mother asked.

"She is majoring in government, you know," I explained. Mother admitted to not having known that, either.

"I won't be able to see her on weekends," I continued, "and I'm going to be very lonely."

Mother's face turned from disinterested to severe. "You are twenty-one years old now, Yulian," she said. "You are a man. You have to behave like a man."

It was then that I pulled the trigger. "I've been thinking about joining the synagogue at Colgate," I said.

I have seen many actors register what is called a double take in the movies, followed by stark terror. Never have I seen one as grandly performed and as totally genuine as Mother's. Her eyes grew round and large; her mouth moved to make sounds but none came. If I had threatened to reveal her blackmail scheme, I couldn't have gotten a stronger reaction.

There was, of course, no synagogue within miles of Colgate. Mother probably suspected—but she also knew when she had been had. She well understood the power I wielded over her. And she was probably, at that moment, even proud of me for daring to wield it. For the first time in my life I had lived up to her image of a man.

Mother took my two hands in hers, tilted her head to one side, and said, "I have an idea, Yulian. Why don't you ask your Susan to marry you this summer?"

That summer, the ROTC program required of me a month's familiarization program at Shaw Air Force Base

in Sumner, North Carolina. We were issued khakis and we
learned to march, make our beds, and clean our barracks
the military way. As a man who would be supporting a wife
on an officer's salary, I took this training very seriously.
With equal seriousness Susan took a secretarial course to
prepare her for office work at Colgate.

Meeting with my mother for tea at Aunt Julia's, Susan's
mother insisted on a church wedding with both a mass
and communion. My mother confessed to her that, pas-
sionately in love, she had married a Jewish man, which
accounted for my un-gentile appearance, but that she and
I were every bit as Catholic as she and Susan. And, as a
matter of fact, she would accept nothing short of mass
and communion for her son since she had been denied it
at her own wedding. How she accounted for her late first
cousin, whose tea it was they were sipping, having been
a prominent Jewish artist well-known in New Canaan, I
don't know. Grandmother sat smiling through the visit
with rosary beads wrapped around her two hands. The
beads must have been a relic of her passing for Catholic
in occupied Poland.

Susan and I visited the priest for premarital counseling
and I was told that I would have to go to confession prior
to the ceremony.

In the confessional, after admitting that it had been so
long since my last confession that I was quite rusty at it,
I confessed to not being as tolerant of stupid people as I
should be. But Father, it seems, was only interested in my
impure thoughts, which I assured him I did not entertain.
"You must have some," the priest said.

There was no way that I was going to admit to what I
thought about alone in bed. I repeated that I did not. As
I left him alone in the confessional I had the feeling that
I had disappointed the old man.

Pierre was my best man. I had chosen Neal, one of my Colgate roommates, but his father turned out to be a Methodist minister, which made Neal unacceptable to Father. The church was filled with relatives of Susan's and friends of my mother. On hand was Spyros Skouras, who had given me my summer job at the Roxy, and Mrs. Skouras, whom Mother referred to as her best friend though I am not sure that it was reciprocated. In home movies of the wedding I've seen Mother introducing my friend Sandra Godowsky to the Skouras's on the church steps. We had the reception at a local inn, where Susan's relatives sat around our head table and mine were on the outer perimeter.

The wedding night was in a hotel in Hartford. The best description would be to say that while we knew the mechanics, neither of us had much of any idea how to proceed.

Our Vetville apartment in Hamilton had a living room, kitchen, bath, and two small bedrooms. The entire apartment was heated by an oil space heater in the little hallway outside the bathroom. Food was refrigerated in an icebox for which the ice man would leave a cake of ice on the back steps every other day and a drain tray which needed to be emptied every twelve hours. I was an old hand at iceboxes. When we went away for a weekend, I would invite a fraternity brother to stay in our apartment and tend to our icebox's needs. Mother saw to it that our own financial needs were taken care of as well.

Adjusting to married life was a cinch for me. The urge to share my life, as I had with Kiki and as, for short moments, I had with my mother, had been with me since Kiki's departure. For the first time since that departure, I now had a bed of which I was more than just the current occupant.

For the first time since I was seven years old, I had a place I could call home.

Then a wrinkle appeared in our plans. The air force announced that only those cadets who signed up for flight training would receive their commissions. With my transatlantic experiences, I had no interest in learning to fly. I had hoped to put in my three years counting blankets and pairs of boots in some supply capacity, but it was not to be. I signed up for pilot training.

When I got my orders some time before graduation, I learned that I would not be reporting for active duty until February of the following year. This was another wrinkle in my plans. How would I support my wife until then?

I remembered Mother's friend Spyros Skouras, president of Twentieth Century-Fox, who had given me my summer job at the Roxy Theater. I went to see him in New York and he told me that when I graduated I should report to a Mr. Sid Rogell at the studio in Los Angeles. He would have a writing job waiting for me. I suspected some communication between Mr. Skouras and Mother had taken place, but I wasn't about to ask questions.

Graduation took place in June in the Colgate Chapel. Mother and Pierre came, bringing a case of champagne. Susan and I had planned a small party on our lawn in conjunction with our neighbors. Mother said she had invited some friends as well. I was dispatched to the bookstore for three dozen Colgate-crested champagne glasses.

My classmates and I marched into the chapel in gowns and mortarboards. Those of us who were being commissioned, a majority of the class, had been told to wear our new class A uniforms under our gowns. Diplomas finally in hand, we marched out onto the quadrangle, removed our robes, and marched back in military splendor. Having been sworn in as air force officers, we marched out a second time, followed by our commencement guests. On the walkway in front of the chapel my wife pinned a gold bar on one of my shoulders while my mother pinned one on the other. Pierre filmed.

In a blue designer dress and a large straw hat, Mother received our guests on the lawn in front of our apartment like an ambassador's wife. The university president and several professors and deans showed up with their wives to chat with my beautiful mother and to wish me well. Pierre filmed and drank Scotch, and Susan and I smiled a lot.

After the party we cleaned up and went our ways: Mother and Pierre to Pierre's new post as consul general in Philadelphia, Susan and I to my new job in Los Angeles.

A week or so later I parked my car, as I had been instructed to do by the guard at the studio gate, and walked into the administration building. The receptionist's station was an old ticket booth from a movie theater. How clever, I thought.

Behind the barred window sat a woman who seemed incongruent with her retro surroundings. With no makeup on, her pale face seemed devoid of features. A T-shirt with horizontal blue and white stripes accented her bosomy figure. She asked about my business in a voice I could barely hear, then made a telephone call. She informed me that someone from Mr. Rogell's office would be with me shortly.

Then, as I waited, an elderly man in a guard's uniform and bedroom slippers came down the hall carrying coffee in a paper cup. As he took the seat that the young woman now vacated, I heard him say, "Thank you, Miss Monroe." The woman gave me a conspiratorial wink as she disappeared down the hall.

My job at the studio was editor, reporter, and photographer of *Action*, the studio magazine. With my Speed Graphic camera I had access to almost anywhere on the lot. I watched Jean Simmons being made up for her role in *Désriée* and passed a football with a bare-chested Marlon Brando as he waited for her. He was playing Napoleon and had on his silk knee breeches and wig. I watched a daytime scene of *The Racers* with Kirk Douglas being shot outdoors at night because, it was explained to me, they could control the light better. I saw the first eight takes of Tom Ewell pulling off his tie and saying one line for *The Seven Year Itch* and heard Ethel Merman belt "There's No Business Like Show Business."

I saw Fred Astaire dancing in *Daddy Longlegs* and Richard Burton spilling his guts in *Prince of Players*. And I actually learned a lot that would stand me well in my own filmmaking career some ten years later. But the best part of that whole Hollywood experience was when Marilyn Monroe noticed me on the *Show Business* set, or *The Seven Year Itch*. Because then she and I would exchange clandestine, conspiratorial winks.

Epilogue

If you find yourself experiencing a certain feeling of unease at this story's ending, that perhaps Julian and Susan do not have the tools to live happily ever after, you are quite correct.

Flying school proved a disaster for me—and, probably, a life saver. While I exhibited fine coordination of the controls, performing takeoffs, turns, banks, stalls, and spins with precision, landings became a nightmare. There are a large number of things you need to watch for in the traffic pattern, such as other airplanes also wanting to land, those taking off on a parallel runway, tower instructions, and the fast-approaching ground. It appeared that I lacked the ability to multitask that this operation required, and I washed out of the program before I could kill myself. Coveting flight pay and the prestige of silver wings on my chest, I applied to navigator school and spent the rest of my air force career as a navigator.

Susan and I proved too young emotionally to be married to each other. Issues arose to which we did not have solutions, my intellectual challenges and writing ambitions major among them. We managed to raise three beautiful daughters, but after a twenty-three-year struggle we went our different ways and have both found happiness.

After my four and a half years in the air force, my
mother introduced me to a little bird of an old lady in
tennis shoes. Her name was Annie Laurie Williams, and she
was the dean of American literary agents. She represented
John Steinbeck, Margaret Mitchell, and Harper Lee among
others, and it was she who had sold *Gone with the Wind*
to David Selznick. Annie Laurie liked the stories I had
written in college and asked me to write a novel for her.

Unprepared, I set to work on one on Cape Cod, where
the air force had deposited me. I struggled for a year and
came up with a manuscript that Annie Laurie couldn't sell.

Then by a stroke of luck I got hired by a television station in Boston to write a series of half-hour documentaries
on the American way of life for the United States Information Agency to distribute throughout the world. This led
to a thirty-five-year career as a writer, director, editor, and
producer of documentary and educational films.

While I was very good at my job and have the awards
to prove it, I also proved to be a terrible businessman and
wage earner. To deal with this fact and the failure of my
first marriage, I underwent numerous bouts of therapy
with analysts, psychologists, and therapists who had me
analyzing my dreams, beating my imagined mother with
old tennis racquets, submitting to hypnosis, and under-
going aroma therapy. None of it seemed to make any
difference.

It wasn't till I was in my sixties and married to Donna,
an incredibly loving and understanding woman, that I
heard a televised discussion on something called Attention Deficit Disorder in Adults. The more that I heard,
the more I recognized my own condition. A psychiatrist
specializing in ADD confirmed my self-diagnosis.

The diagnosis of ADD combined with dyslexia explained
my inattention in school and part of the reason for the ter-

rible self-image I subsequently developed. It also explained the business ineptitude that had driven Susan up the wall.

I closed my little film production business and turned to what I did best, writing. After a series of books on photography, computer operation, dealing with angry customers, and Franklin and Eleanor Roosevelt, I sat down to write the story of my mother's and my escape from occupied Poland. Published in 2006 as *Mother and Me: Escape from Warsaw 1939*, the book was named Book of the Year by *ForeWord* magazine. Two sequels, *A Ship in the Harbor* and *Loves of Yulian*, followed, and this book completes the series.

Professor Jonathan Kistler, his wife, Patricia, daughter Tasha (who won't know about the role she played in my adolescent life until she reads this), and her sisters, Tammy, Tessie, and Patti all became family friends of mine through all three of my marriages. We exchanged numerous visits, and Jon and Pat continued reading my unpublished stories and encouraging me not to give up. At the wedding to my present wife, Donna, Patricia sat in the front pew in the role of mother of the groom while her aged husband recovered from a boisterous rehearsal dinner. I miss them both.

As for Mother, her life became beautiful when they moved to Philadelphia. Mother had finally managed to convince the French government that they owed Pierre for his documented heroism in the African campaign. They agreed to open a consulate general in Philadelphia with Pierre at its head if she would support it with her private income.

She and Pierre rented a townhouse, hired a French chef, a butler, and a maid, and entertained royally. They became close friends with the family of actress and princess Grace Kelly, the Walter Annenbergs, and numerous other pillars of Philadelphia society. In their Philadelphia home, Susan and I, on leave from the air force, would meet the

likes of Pearl Buck, Edith Piaf, Burgess Meredith, Eugene
Ormandy, Marcel Marceau, and many other stars of business, government, and the arts. She seemed to have recon-
ciled herself to my Hebraic nose except when somebody
whom Mother considered an anti-Semite was invited to
dinner. Then Susan and I were given money to eat out.

Pierre charmed Philadelphia society, and Mother was
in the society pages on a regular basis. On her many trips
to Paris Mother was introduced to couturiers Yves Saint
Laurent and Hubert de Givenchy, who gave Mother outfits
to model in Philadelphia and New York. Returning home,
Mother would lend them to her dressmaker to copy for
her customers. Pierre joined Susan and me in trying to
tell Barbara that this was not ethical, but Mother did not
seem to care. Photographed often wearing her Dior and
Balenciaga originals, Mother's ten years in Philadelphia
were the happiest of her life.

Then Pierre's Scotch and Chesterfields caught up to him
and he died of throat cancer, but not before being honored
by the French government and his many American friends
in one very moving medal ceremony in the Philadelphia
home. Widowed, Mother moved to New York and rented
a grand apartment on Park Avenue.

But no longer the wife of the consul general, no longer
seeing herself as young and beautiful, Mother tragically
came under the influence of drugs prescribed for her by
a collection of unwitting and unscrupulous doctors. I had
my own filmmaking office in New York at the time, and I
tried to keep Mother on an even keel with daily telephone
calls and frequent visits. At one point I had her agree to
go see a therapist until she called to tell me that at a lun-
cheon with literary agent Annie Laurie Williams she had
agreed to write another memoir. "I don't need a therapist
anymore," she said. "I'm going to be famous."

Her longtime latent disapproval of Susan blossomed into mutual hatred. Mother would no longer visit us and her grandchildren in Westport, Connecticut. In New York, she would pick fights with my secretary and my assistants. When she invited me to lunch, there would usually be some attractive single woman for me to meet.

When she realized that I wasn't following up on these introductions Mother grew angry. When one day I refused to interrupt a filming session to escort her to her hairdresser appointment, something Mother had been managing successfully without me on a weekly basis, she began spreading the rumor that I was gay. When on my orders Hilda, my secretary, refused to interrupt my conference with a client for a phone call from Mother, my mother threatened to contact Hilda's mother and tell her she was having an affair with her boss. I finally got Mother off Hilda's back by playing my blackmail card for the second and last time, threatening to write Pierre's mother in France and tell her that her daughter-in-law was Jewish.

Finally, Mother made her exit on her own terms and in her own style, at the age of sixty-two. In the middle of the night during an argument with a younger escort, she flew out of her thirteenth-story window onto Park Avenue in her flowing nightgown. At her funeral in a Catholic cemetery in Connecticut there were people who cried, including the wife of her apartment building super, and people who came to dance on her grave.

My uncle, Arthur Szyk, has enjoyed a revival in recent years. An Arthur Szyk Society has been formed with a website displaying many of his beautiful illuminations, illustrations, and those venomous caricatures. Books and articles about his unique artistry have appeared in numerous languages. Exhibitions celebrating his art, his compassion, and his patriotic spirit have recently been held in Washington, Poland, Germany, Japan, and Israel.

My Rumsey roommate Rod Hodgins, whose father had turned him into two little girls in his book, went on to Harvard where he roomed with a kid named Ted Kennedy who, Rod claimed, was the dumbest roommate he ever had. "The guy went and got himself kicked out of school." Rod became an industrial psychologist and passed away from cancer some thirty years ago.

In recent years, after a long silence, I have revisited Rumsey Hall. The school had moved from its cramped campus in Cornwall, Connecticut, to a new location in the town of Washington. The old campus stood deserted and desolate, and I found that satisfying. The twisted floorboards, broken glass, and rotted nails seemed a fitting condition for the place. Nature was reclaiming what I believed to have been an aberrant institution.

I think that my greatest grievance against Rumsey is that they calloused my sensitivity. Yes, I learned not to complain about the small problems in life, but I also learned to expect the same of others. It became particularly troublesome when I had small children and did not take their feelings as seriously as I now believe I should have done. My past callousness haunts me today as I recall myself unwittingly channeling the Rumsey director in dealing with perceived transgressions.

It took me a few years to accept the new Rumsey Hall as having any meaning in my life. I knew neither the place nor the people. If it was anything like the old school, I would have preferred to see it removed from the educational system. And if it was all different, then what claim did it have on me?

Yet, something kept calling. I have visited the new campus and been impressed with facilities that would rival a small college. I have also met with the new staff and alumni, seen something of the new curriculum, and viewed many, many photographs of the new students. There is an air of professionalism here that was clearly missing from the old school. The students, almost ten times the number of my old schoolmates, seem happy. In place of the burdened faces of my memory and newly rediscovered yearbooks, I see a glow of health and enthusiasm. I see an experience I wish I had had for myself.

Today, I live in a 112-year-old house in Stamford, Connecticut, with my lovely wife, Donna. Between us we have five children and, at last count, nine grandchildren and two great-grands.

In the study of this old house I have created a world where it is I who gets to say what happens and to whom: I have become a published novelist. Like my Uncle Arthur, my weapon of choice is humor, and I have created a village named Venice on the coast of Massachusetts, based on the village of Pocasset on Cape Cod where I struggled to write my first novel some fifty years ago. I've peopled it with characters based on persons I have known or would like to have known.

I have inflicted my protagonist, Kip, with many of my own misfortunes and character flaws and then watched him work his way out from under them. Arriving in Venice in his seventies after a life in which his bread always landed jam-side down, Kip meets the delectable postmistress and sculptor Amanda and finally learns to live and to love. The lovely, creative but also creatively accident-prone Amanda was inspired by my late second wife, Phyllis.

The first novel, *Writer's Block*, was published in 2010, but when I had finished writing it I found that I missed Kip and Amanda and their loopy Venice friends. So I sat down and wrote a sequel, *The Best Sunset in Venice*. Then I let Kip and Amanda romp through *A Scandal in Venice*, in which Amanda tries to reconcile Kip with his deceased mother and finds the woman more than she can handle, and *Alexander's Part-Time Band*, in which Kip's boarding school roommate shows up and recalls memories better left forgotten.

Because book publishing today leaves much of a book's promotion to its author, I give talks in libraries, universities, churches, and synagogues. On my daily runs along Stamford's Hope Street I carry a pocketful of fliers proclaiming my books and press them on unsuspecting people I encounter. This includes other runners or walkers who make the mistake of waving a friendly greeting, drivers stopped at stop signs, and homeowners gardening too close to the road. For these efforts, I have been dubbed the Hope Street Stalker and now write a blog entitled Confessions of the Hope Street Stalker. In it I recount the adventures I encounter on these runs and the thoughts and ideas that pop into my head.

Sometimes on these runs I meet someone who has actually read one of my books. These become highly emotional moments for me and passing motorists are then treated to the sight of two people in running shorts hugging each other alongside the road.

Thank you for your interest.